UNDERSTANDING THE PROFILES IN HUMAN DESIGN

THE FACILITATOR'S GUIDE TO UNLEASHING
POSSIBILITY

ROBIN WINN, MFT

Cover design: Jennifer Stimson

Editor: Erika Roman Saint-Pierre

Photo Credit: Juliet Jarmosco

ADVANCE PRAISE

"Robin is so methodical and thorough in this Profiles' book. Although very much a resource guide for professionals, this book captivated me as a summer novel would! I found myself reading about my loved ones as if I was being brought to a new angle and perspective of their profiles. Reading my own profile was also an insightful and enlightening process of finding gems of how my profile is perceived by my colleague & friend. It is wonderfully written and a resource for my Human Design Library."

— **ASHA D RAMAKRISHNA**, CERTIFIED QUANTUM HUMAN DESIGN™ SPECIALIST, BEST-SELLING AUTHOR OF *THE PRIESTESS CODE: AWAKENING THE MODERN WOMAN,* AND FOUNDER OF *SACRED COMMERCE & MODERN PRIESTESS SCHOOL*

"In *Understanding the Profiles in Human Design: The Facilitator's Guide to Unleashing Potential,* Robin Winn's warm, conversational style takes a complex topic and makes it easy to understand. Throughout the text, her incorporation of personal stories keeps the information relatable and the reader engaged. As a Quantum Human Design™ Specialist myself, I began this book anticipating to encounter familiar information. I am thrilled to share how wrong I was!

As is Robin's gift, she once again shares a rich and unique perspective of Human Design, this time through her exploration of the Profiles. Throughout my experience with this book, I repeatedly referenced my own chart, as well as those of several of my clients, seeing the information in a beautiful and empowering new light. Once again Robin has crafted a valuable resource that promises to not only become a go-to guide for Human Design professionals, but also an enlightening text for anyone wishing to learn more of the deep truths about themselves."

— **CARI WISE**, DVM, MA ED, CERTIFIED QUANTUM HUMAN DESIGN™ SPECIALIST, CERTIFIED LIFE COACH AND FOUNDER OF *ALIGNED HUMAN DESIGN.*

"We are living in a time of great disruption. Evolution requires change and change can be difficult and unsettling. It is more important than ever to know yourself, understand yourself, and uncover your gifts so you can ground yourself and better navigate this evolution. Robin shares the profiles in an easy to understand and usable way that brings one a deep knowledge of themselves without the need for a deep study of the rich and complex system we call Human Design.

Whether practitioner collaborating with clients or student, this book is an invaluable tool with the best explanation of the profiles and how to use them that I have seen."

"Robin Winn has done us the extraordinary service of giving us a clear and cogent understanding of a vital aspect of the Human Design system, the Profiles. The Profiles are like the characters we play in life, and Robin has described them with such care and clarity that we can recognize ourselves and each other in her words. At the same time, she cautions us against ever using this system to typecast people, noting that this would be anathema to the core principles of Human Design. Not only this, her chapters on how to use this information with clients guide us with true-to-life examples so we can see and feel the profiles as living beings rather than mere constructs. This work makes Human Design accessible and valuable to anyone who works with people and wants to know and love them more deeply."

"If you are looking for a book of wisdom on Human Design - this one is it! When I was first introduced to Human Design, I was fascinated with how well Robin Winn pinpointed the root cause of why I was feeling inadequate and questioning my intelligence and the ability to be successful. I was trying to act as a Generator and my Manifestor self was confused and frustrated. Then, Ms. Winn explained my 3/5 Profile, and everything fell immediately into place. She described me to a T! I could now celebrate my gifts of *trial and error* versus cursing that I was a failure. Soon after, I became a student of Ms. Winn's, knowing this body of knowledge would be transformational for my grief coaching clients. But I must admit, learning Human Design was a bit over-whelming. There were so many layers to wrap my head around, and it wasn't until I learned and understood the Profiles that I finally tapped into the powerful knowledge of Human Design. This book will definitely be the first thing I grab now when I am working with my clients!"

— **PAT SHEVELAND**, RN, PCC, ICF CERTIFIED LIFE COACH, GRIEF COACH, QIGONG TEACHER, BEST-SELLING AUTHOR OF *THE CONFIDENT GRIEF COACH: A GUIDE FOR HELPING CLIENTS PROCESS LOSS,* AND FOUNDER OF THE *CONFIDENT GRIEF COACH SCHOOL*

"*Understanding the Profiles in Human Design* is a must read for coaches and teachers as well as those who truly desire one of the secrets to understanding themselves and the world we live in.

If you are on the journey to determine who you are and what your real purpose in life is, Robin Winn is a master teacher who has the uncanny ability with her writing to give you tools to be confident that you are taking the right road. By explaining the two numbers of one's Profile in the vast Human Design system, Robin expertly yet simply brings us knowledge of ourselves and those around us. She has taken a system that some find very complex and made it accessible, usable, and relatable by providing entertaining vignettes of real people (some quite famous that she has personally worked with) along with easy-to-understand images and explanations.

As a physician, intuitive, and relationship coach (and 5/1 Splenic Projector), learning the pieces of Human Design from Robin has transformed my relationships with my husband, family, and colleagues. In addition, the teachings in this book (as well as her other books) have allowed me to become a truly transformational coach for my clients by making available user-friendly and short explanations in an area that has until now been largely confusing, woo-woo mumbo jumbo.

Possessing the knowledge that Human Design Profiles provide regarding conscious and unconscious strength and vulnerabilities that we are all born with and how to actually *use* this information about Profiles is, quite frankly, game changing."

— **VERONICA ANDERSON**, MD, INTUITIVE
GUIDE & RELATIONSHIP COACH, FOUNDER OF
THE R.E.S.P.E.C.T METHOD ™, AND BEST-SELLING
AUTHOR OF *GET THE RESPECT YOU DESERVE: 7
SECRETS TO GETTING SEEN AND HEARD IN YOUR
JOB AND RELATIONSHIPS*

"Robin Winn's third book *Understanding the Profiles in Human Design* gives those of us who are wisdom seekers the next puzzle piece on our Human Design Adventure.

Robin again takes us on an enchanting journey based on her exquisite perspective, experience, and well-selected stories to explore the hidden treasure of our Profiles.

I found it hard to resist to looking up my own Profile first before exploring the profiles of my family, friends, and clients.

This is a great book to help parents let their children thrive, to help leaders to unfold the potential of their diverse team members, and to help authors and film-makers get a new twist on blowing life into the archetypes of their stories.

At last, this is a book that helps us understand how we learn and navigate the human being that we are. It helps us to embrace, tolerate, and be at peace with people that are different from us.

The world needs all of us in our vital spectrum and on the level of our highest potential.

This is what this book is truly about. Love It!"

— **IRIS SENG**, BUSINESS STORY ARCHITECT, CERTIFIED HUMAN DESIGN CONSULTANT AND PRACTITIONER

"Get ready to dog-ear and highlight page after page of this treasure of the profiles by Robin Winn. I found it to be a page-turner! Even when my husband called that lunch was on the table, I couldn't put it down (and he's a good cook). The thing is, I felt seen. I could see others. I felt met. It felt good to comprehend why I am the way I am. *Understanding the Profiles in Human Design* is a simple, succulent grasp of an otherwise complex delineation of our puzzle piece in life. Robin's articulate, intimate reflection of the Profiles makes Human Design sparkle and come alive!"

— **HEIDI WINN,** LMHC, SACRED LISTENING
COACH AND THERAPIST, CERTIFIED HUMAN
DESIGN CONSULTANT AND PRACTITIONER

"I find the work Robin Winn brings forth incredibly insightful and would enhance any healing or spiritual practice. Robin manages to take several ancient practices, molding them into one comprehensive modern approach. Self-awareness is the cornerstone for personal growth, and it enhances one's ability to work with others. This work is a must for healers, therapists, spiritual practitioners, seekers on a spiritual path, and those who wish to excel in the business world. It is a phenomenal tool for the seasoned professional and the beginner looking for the next step.
What a blessing!"

— **GREG TOEWS**, CEO / PRESIDENT OF ASTARA
SPIRITUAL ORGANIZATION, OWNER OF PLANT
PRANA ESSENTIAL OILS, CONSULTANT

CONTENTS

To my beloved wife, Yarrow.
Sharing our lives has been a journey of tumultuous transformation, deep pleasure, and unexpected grace.
I am so grateful to walk this path with you – my 6/2 soulmate.
In love and gratitude for your exquisite presence,

Your 6/2 beloved, Robin

FOREWORD

Robin Winn and I first met through the Author Incubator, a coaching program designed to help authors write their books. She became one of their most successful authors. Over weekly zoom calls with the group, I was captivated by Robin's amazing energy. It seemed like everyone in the program had signed up for her Human Design readings. They were praising the insights gained, and it made me curious. Each week, someone new would discuss their incredible reading with Robin and how it positively affected their business and how they approached their clients. I knew through some preliminary quiz that I was a Manifesting Generator but until then, I had no desire to learn more. Robin changed that for me. How was it possible that a simple reading could be so impactful?

Curiosity got the best of me, and I finally set up a reading. Besides, I would get some one-on-one time with Robin. When the day came, I was excited. She sent my chart in advance, which was a complete a mystery. It seemed a bizarre configuration of squiggles and lines. In case you haven't seen your chart, it looks peculiar. I was intrigued about what it all meant. When we finally began our session, I felt her radiate light and calm. Robin used a cursor to explain the chart, and somehow when she was outlining my Centers and Channels, I felt a transmission of energy. It was as though the chart came alive. I didn't always understand what she was saying, but I knew that I felt seen and understood. I felt a heart activation.

Robin confirmed that I was a Manifesting Generator. She explained that I had a 4/1 Profile and an Open Emotional Solar Plexus Center among other things. As she was sharing how this information affects me, she was also holding space for me to feel the full expression of my chart. This experience was even more profound than the chart analysis. I could feel I was resonating on a higher frequency. Robin was a conduit accessing my chart and making it come alive. This created a positive vision where I was able to internalize this information which gave me even more confidence in who I am. I know this is only one of Robin's gifts. She can translate information on a whole other level. She brings out the most positive aspects of the chart and leans into them as she sees the challenges as opportunities.

After the reading, I wanted to learn more about the Centers and the Profiles. I was hoping to find a book or more information on the Internet. No luck. There was very little out there. Robin serendipitously answered the call by focusing first on the Centers in her second book, *Understanding the Centers in Human Design* and now the Profiles in this current book, *Understanding the Profiles in Human Design*. It's as though she can't write fast enough to answer the many questions that are posed when studying the chart. She tells us so much more.

Later, it would come to pass that Robin and I did an exchange where she took my class, Meet Your Guides, and I took her basic class in Learning Human Design. I channel a group of entities called the *Light Beings* and I was teaching how to connect with Spirit and access past life experiences, as well as how to access the

Archangels and Ascended Masters. These connections are available to everyone. My class came first, and I was thrilled to have Robin's energy and expertise. The class was an eight-week course dedicated to connecting with one's spiritual team of guides and becoming more receptive to their messages. Before each class, I offered a meditation to create alignment with the individual class members and to raise the frequency and vibration of the space. During this time, I surrounded the group with protection and light.

At that moment during our first meditation, sitting with the guides where I have a more elevated perspective, I could see the incredible spiritual resources available to Robin. The guides were ready to download more information about Human Design. Robin was right there on the precipice of activating more details and a new perspective. It was as though Ra Uru Hu, the founder of Human Design, was whispering in her ears. Robin had/has an entire circle of guides at her disposal. As she started to access the information, she started tapping into this huge reserve of knowledge. I've watched as this relationship with her guides has only grown.

In actualizing her purpose, Robin's personal journey has led her to this moment where she is able to transmit information about Human Design that hasn't been shared before. She recognizes that the chart is in fact a launching pad and not the end result for the individual. Each chart incorporates potential. It shares the individual puzzle piece that connects each of us to a greater whole and our contribution to the planet. The chart is not a finite piece of information but instead a valuable tool for transformation.

By understanding our Profile, we are taking our own Human Design to an even more refined view of who we are. This information will not only deepen our own understanding but present more detailed material for your clients as well. Robin is now communicating information that hasn't been received before and accessing even more subtleties of the design chart to be shared with all of us.

This contribution to humanity will impact each of you in a profound way. It is through the Profiles that you can begin to understand your learning path and open to your potential as you recognize your strengths and your challenges. Again, this isn't finite, but it is all about what is possible and how you are able to express yourself more fully. Robin continues to isolate different aspects of Human Design by channeling her own guidance and being receptive to the energies that understand this system in an insightful way.

Robin is a conduit for activating light codes as well using Human Design as her vehicle for transmission. Her entire life has culminated in this moment of expression. Many of these activations are subtle and imperceptible, creating change and shifts in thinking even without us realizing it.

I have never met anyone who works as diligently at personal development. Robin's dedication to her life process and commitment to growing and expanding in every arena is an inspiration. Robin's information can be trusted. She is also rooted in her heart center, which brings deep compassion. She is a difference maker positively affecting everyone she touches.

The information presented here is another incredible resource. As a channel, I am used to seeing things from an energetic point of view. Human Design can seem quite linear. Robin changes that perspective by incorporating energy and harmonics instead of just laying out a factual account.

The information in this book about the Profiles is juicy and fun. At the same time, it gives so much substantive data. I have read the chapter on my 4/1 Profile over and over. Each time I receive something new. I know that as you read Robin's words, each of you will experience a new way of interpreting your Human Design through your Profiles. I am excited for your journey. With Robin you have a trusted guide for the material and further exploration into your chart.

— **DEBORAH SUDARSKY**, M.ED. MASTER
INTUITIVE COACH, BEST-SELLING AUTHOR OF
*EMBRACE YOUR PSYCHIC GIFTS: THE GUIDE TO
SPIRITUAL AWAKENING, AND MEET YOUR GUIDES.*

1

YOU WANT TO KNOW MORE
ABOUT THE PROFILES?

As I contemplated writing this, my third Human Design book, I thought about you. Who are you? What are your challenges? Why would you be drawn to read a book on the Human Design Profiles? What do you need?

At this time in history, our needs are shifting. We've entered a cycle of disruption. The world is in flux. We are facing unprecedented challenges.

On the global level, we're standing on unsteady ground. Will the Earth survive climate change? Will disruptions in the supply chain impact our access to goods? Will the pandemic continue to unravel travel, jobs, and life as we've known it? Will divisive politics destroy our humanitarian bond?

On a personal level, we are reassessing our lives, our work, and our relationships. What truly matters? Will we be taken down by the changes? Or will we rise up and meet them? How do we go forward from an empowered place? How do we support our family, our friends, our colleagues, and our clients to face the influx of changes?

If you're picking up this book, you're drawn to Human Design. You're curious about this system. Maybe it can offer support. Perhaps you're hoping it can help you in your life, in your work, and in your relationships. You want something pragmatic and usable. You want the Profiles explained in a way that is easily understandable and makes sense. You want them to make a difference in your life. The possibility that the Profiles could unleash your potential and your client's potential sparks you.

But where do you start?

Human Design can seem so hard to grasp. So complex. It would be easy to dismiss it. I know I did initially.

I'm guessing you're like me, and you've studied many other tools to assess people: Meyers Briggs, Enneagram, and DISC, to name a few. You appreciate them. They are helpful. They are good. But there is something in the Human Design system that speaks to you at another level.

My friend and mentor Greg Toews says, "It's magical. It takes ancient wisdom and brings it to modern times." I couldn't agree more.

Human Design is so much more than another personality assessment tool. Maybe you already know that. Maybe you've studied the Types and Authority. Maybe you've read my book on The Centers. Maybe you're already using Human Design with your clients. Maybe you're aware that Human Design is here to help humanity evolve.

Or maybe you're newer to Human Design. Maybe this is your first foray. Either way, you are here now.

In Human Design, we say the system, or the Triangle, calls the people to it who are meant to use it. If you're picking up this book, you are one of the called.

Now is the time. Now is the time for you to understand the Profiles. Now is the time to use this knowledge to help you and your clients be more aligned. Now is the time to learn to navigate challenges even more skillfully. Now is the time to recognize our differences so that we can support each other's contributions. Now is the time to come together to respect and call on our unique authentic selves as an inherent part of the solution in these disruptive times. Now is the time to unleash our potential.

So, here we are.

Embarking on a journey together.

You, me, and the Profiles.

2

A LOVER OF HUMAN DESIGN

It makes sense to know something about the person you're traveling with when you set off on a journey. Why are they traveling this path? What's the destination?

The first thing you should know about me is that I am a lover of Human Design.

When Human Design showed up in a way that I could truly comprehend, everything changed. I saw myself in a new light. I saw my clients in a new light. I saw the world in a new light. You could say it was a homecoming. I was welcomed into the family of humanity. I was seen. I belonged. Exactly as I was. For the first time, I understood that my unique self was integral to the unfolding evolution.

But that was just the beginning. With the light turned on, I saw that everyone belonged. Each person, in their full uniqueness, mattered. They were essential to the whole.

There is a simple metaphor that landed this understanding for me. In Human Design, we are all pieces of the puzzle of humanity. There are roughly 8 billion of us. Each one of us is perfectly designed. We each have a unique, multi-dimensional blueprint. When we live the possibility of that blueprint, we fulfill our dharma. We thrive.

ENTELECHY

Entelechy is a Greek word meaning *the realization of potential*. An acorn realizes its potential when it becomes an oak tree. That is its entelechy. Each of us has a unique entelechy. As we live this entelechy, we bring the gifts we were designed to give. There is no hierarchy – just as there is no hierarchy in nature. A redwood tree isn't more valuable than an oak tree. A rose isn't more valuable than a daffodil. Though we might assign more value to something, the inherent value is equal. Each of our puzzle pieces combine to create the wonder and magnificence of the whole. Problems arise when:

• we don't know our puzzle piece

• we don't understand our inherent value

• we are conditioned to believe there are hierarchies of value

• we attempt to live puzzle pieces other than our own to establish value

• we fail and blame ourselves, believing we are deficient.

This could look something like: *I don't know my purpose. I don't have anything to offer. I've got to do it the way they're telling me to, even though it doesn't feel right. I can't get it right. There's something wrong with me.* Unless you're living in alignment with yourself, you will be caught in the web of some version of this misunderstanding.

The devastating result is that we suffer, and all humanity loses out. We don't bring our gifts. Our unique light stays hidden. We don't realize our entelechy. Our potential lies dormant. Our purpose is unlived.

Don't get me wrong, it's not always easy to live your purpose, especially when most of us were taught we had to be someone other than who we were. It takes letting go of the concepts and conditioning. It takes standing up, showing up, and being different than the status quo. Depending on your chart, it might mean letting yourself learn by making mistakes or honoring your impulse to *hermit*.

Living your purpose requires listening to your inner guidance rather than listening to what others are telling you. Ultimately, it means being on your own behalf. It means being committed to your authenticity. As my friend Pali Summerlin says, "It's a high bar."

Definitely risky business. The stakes are high. That said, the cost of not living our entelechy is higher. In Anaïs Nin's words:

"And the day came when the risk to remain tight in a bud was more painful than the risk it took to blossom."

The cost of not living our entelechy is our personal health, wealth, vitality, and wellbeing. Our *joie de vivre*. Look around and see the malaise, the discontent, and the ennui. Feel your own knowing that there is more to you. Can you recognize the unbearable awareness that you are unrealized? Now, think of your clients and their suffering. Trapped like Sisyphus, they roll boulders up a hill only to have them slide back down as they near the top.

Not realizing our potential is crushing. Suicide is the 10th leading cause of death in the United States. The American Dream is no longer enough. Fulfilling an image of who we should be, do, or have ultimately leaves us empty.

Even more cataclysmic – and yes these are dramatic words, fit for the potentially perilous situation of our times – is the cost of humanity as a whole not understanding and calling forth the entelechy of each person. This habit of neglecting our essential selves has got to stop.

We are at a turning point. We have the chance to step into a new paradigm as the old structure collapses. We cannot do it as individuals. We must do it together. But not together from a homogenized pattern. Together, living our unique entelechy.

It is in this way, we honor and live our brilliance. We recognize and honor the brilliance of each other. When we are connected to our inner guidance, we get the information we need. And then, the as-yet-unrealized solutions come forth.

Basically, what we're saying is that the world as we know it is on a collision course, and it takes each one of us living our entelechy to change that trajectory. We are being called to move into partnership with ourselves, with each other, and with life.

FROM DISSOCIATION TO EMBODIMENT

Think of it this way.

As a kid, I was pretty dissociated. It was my survival strategy. In terms of my Human Design chart, I could explain it by saying my Conscious Moon is in Gate 20, called *The Now*. This energy is a driving force in my life. Only, I was mostly living the low side of that energy, I wanted to be as far away from The Now (and my entelechy) as I could get. The world was not comfortable. I was not in my body. All my focus was external. I was trying to figure out how to fit in. I was definitely thinking I should be someone else's puzzle piece. Mine was clearly deficient.

In the moments I did drop into my body – often in meditation or lovemaking, sometimes while I wrote poetry – I had access to worlds I couldn't explain. Images, sensations, an immediate exhilaration, and a threatening aliveness flooded my system. You could say I had a love/hate relationship with *The Now* energy.

As I became a young adult, the world, which is always looking for ways to support us, put Marion Rosen and Rosen Method Bodywork in my path. I have that inner sense that when I resonate with something, I do it, no matter how odd it might seem to the conventional world. Raised to believe I should be someone recognizably important, I chose instead to become a Rosen Method bodyworker.

Being present for other people was a survival skillset I'd mastered. Being present to myself? That was another story. Being touched in a gentle way that met my tension without activating my defenses broke me open. As I felt myself reflected in someone's hands, my defenses melted. It was not pretty. Everything I had so carefully kept myself from feeling was displayed in full force. I was not prepared for Pandora's box to fly open.

I began therapy to make sense of the mess. Then, I spent a good twenty years sorting through the *mishegas*. With the help of bodywork, therapy, meditation, qigong, and inquiry, I found my way back into my body.

So, why am I saying all of this? What relevance does it have to Human Design, entelechy, and the trajectory of the world? I think my path replicates humanity's path. As a people, as a culture, and as a world, we have not lived our entelechy. We have tried to escape who we are individually because it can be so threatening to the tribe.

For many of us, if we did not conform as children, we risked losing the support of the people we were dependent on. We took this experience into adulthood. We abandoned ourselves to ensure love and survival. We dissociated from our inner guidance. From our potential. From our connection to nature. From our connection to each other. And most importantly, we dissociated from the power of our earthy, humanly existence as embodied spirit in partnership with Source.

The world is hitting that place I hit on the bodywork table. We're seeing the mess. We can no longer hide out. We can no longer live separated from the truth of who we are.

It's time to know who we are and claim it. It's time to show up and let our differences shed new light. We cannot solve the current problems while we're absent from ourselves.

Marion described Rosen Method: "This work is about transformation from the person you think you are to the person you really are."

We have been living the person we think we are or think we are supposed to be. It's time to discover who we really are. This is the portal that awaits us. This is the gift Human Design brings. We're looking at a radical shift from groupthink to individual expression. It's a huge shift with enormous, unprecedented potential.

HUMAN DESIGN AS A *TERMA*

I often talk about Human Design as a *terma*. In Tibetan Buddhism, a *terma* is a hidden treasure. *Termas* are esoteric teachings that were buried by awakened masters in earlier centuries. The intent of *termas* is to reveal these teachings at an auspicious time to support humanity's evolution.

The teachings of Human Design were transmitted through light *beings*. We could say the *terma* was revealed through light. A Canadian fellow, now known as Ra Uru Hu, was the *tertön*, the receiver of the teaching. Sometimes called the reluctant mystic, Ra was on retreat off the Coast of Spain during the Harmonic Convergence in 1987. When he returned to his cabin, he found it was filled with light *beings*. These *beings* spent days transmitting the intricate Human Design teachings. The *beings* said that this information was here to support the evolution of humanity. It was for everyone, but especially for parents to aid in parenting their children. Think about it. If a child is seen as an individual and knows who they are, a different path lies ahead. If their entelechy is called forth from the beginning…imagine what might be possible.

Human Design is so much more than a tool. It is an esoteric teaching made for our times. It is the light showing the way forward. Both at an individual and a collective level, Human Design reveals the necessity and the utility of living our differentiation. It ushers in a new understanding and a higher level of coherence.

See why I'm a lover of Human Design? It brings new light infused with unprecedented possibility for us individually and as a world. It awakens kindness and respect for difference. It calls forth greatness.

WHY A BOOK ON THE PROFILES?

This is the third book I've written on Human Design. I wrote the first one on Type, Strategy, and Authority: *Understanding Your Clients through Human Design: The Breakthrough Technology*. Type, Strategy, and Authority are the foundation of Human Design. They are the major puzzle pieces. Simply knowing them, you have a treasure trove of information that can help you know yourself, your loved ones, and your clients in ways that can be life altering.

My second book was a passion book: *Understanding the Centers in Human Design: The Facilitator's Guide to Transforming Pain into Possibility*. This was a foray into the Open and Defined Centers as a way to understand our strengths and challenges in life. Deep and rich, this book sheds light on who we are and our propensity to have mistaken beliefs about ourselves. It is filled with tools to help you sort out and work with some of those misunderstandings.

Truly, it would have made the most sense to write the second book on the Profiles. There is a kind of no-nonsense pragmatism to the Profiles. They are easy to understand, and, well, fun to learn. When I give workshops on the Profiles, the level of engagement intensifies. People's curiosity wakes up. Something clicks.

In a way, the Profiles can stand alone. You don't have to study a lot of Human Design to work with them. They're easy to access. They're a great starting place for coaches or people wanting to begin using Human Design with people. They also add a level of depth to people already familiar with Human Design.

Wherever you are on your Human Design journey, the Profiles will be a wonderful addition. The Profiles give us the key to how we're meant to do what we're here to do. Living in alignment with your profile can be the difference between thriving and struggling.

I know that Human Design can be challenging to learn. People always tell me that it's such a complex system. I want to argue with them, tell them they are wrong, or dissuade them.

But I remember my first reading in 2004. My eyes glazed over. My brain went on tilt. There was so much information, and it was all too much to process. There was the bodygraph with all these colors and shapes and numbers. There were all these different parts: Type, Strategy, Authority, Circuitry, Centers, Gates, Channels, Planets, Definition, and yes, Profiles. It was woo-woo even for me at the time.

It wasn't until 2013 that I was called to study Human Design in earnest. At that point, new material on Human Design became available to read and the ability for people to run charts opened up. A switch turned on inside me. I was ready. Like a sponge, I learned everything I could about Human Design. The information was downloading into me. I quickly understood the basics. But the deeper training began with real life experience.

I began by running everyone's chart I knew. I come from a large family, so my parents and six siblings were an obvious beginning. And I ran all my friends' charts in an attempt to better understand them. Then I began running my clients' charts. I would sit in session with their chart on the table beside me, week after week, year after year. Our work shifted because of the chart and the light it brought to their lives. Human Design brought a new dimension, a new way of understanding trauma. It brought in a higher level of consciousness to our work.

As I helped my clients connect to the energy of their charts, they began to see themselves with more clarity and the trajectory of their lives shifted. It was through this process of being intimately involved with the charts in relation to people's lived lives that my understanding of Human Design solidified. The more I understood from hands-on experience, the clearer and easier it became to understand and comprehend the Human Design system. I learned and worked with Human Design not so much from an intellectual, informational context, but from a relational, psychological, and spiritual context. I was looking at suffering and the freedom from suffering. I was looking at how can people be more aligned with their authentic selves.

It is from this organic process that the depth of my Human Design knowledge was born. I was always one with a keen interest in understanding people. Over the years, I had dabbled in a variety of systems. I started by studying Astrology, Numerology, and Meyer's Briggs. Then, later, as a graduate student in psychology, I delved into the study of character based on the DSM (Diagnostic Statistical Manual).

But it was the Enneagram that was my true love. My first introduction began in an aikido class in 1985. The Enneagram was all the rage in Berkeley at the time. There were panels on the different Enneatypes. Everyone was talking Types. I read every book I could get my hands on and set out to understand my family and friends through that lens. As I became a Rosen Method bodywork practitioner, then a psychotherapist, I incorporated the use of the Enneagram as a source of guidance in my work with clients. In 2000, I began a twenty-year course of study in the Diamond Approach with Faisal Muqaddam. With Faisal, my understanding of the Enneagram went to new levels and became the bedrock of my understanding of and work with clients.

I love the Enneagram and continue to use it to this day in my attempt to understand and work with people. It is a brilliant system to recognize our ego patterns. It shows us who we are not. It lays out the strategies we've adopted to navigate trauma.

Human Design, as I keep pointing out, is different. It's in a category all on its own. As I said, it is a transmission. It was transmitted to us by light *beings,* and it carries a transmission. Merriam-Webster defines transmission as: "an act, process, or instance of transmitting: something that is transmitted: Message."

Human Design is a message. It carries a frequency. When you tap into the frequency the message is available. While the left-brain information is necessary as the doorway to the transmission, the real power is accessed as you make direct contact with the frequency. Whether you choose to work with it at that level, or not, is up to you.

When we're talking about the Profiles, we're talking about six lines. Each line tells a story. Each line emits an energy. Each line holds essential information to help us unlock our entelechy. In pairs, the lines create the Profiles. The invitation in this book is:

• to understand the left-brain information

• to reveal the story of each Line and each of the Profiles

• to access the energy, the transmission, of each of the Lines and Profiles

• to use this transmission to activate you and your client's potential

MY PROFILE

I'm what is called a 6/2 Profile in Human Design. How accurately this describes me is a bit uncanny. Just with these two numbers and the information they reflected, I felt seen and understood at a new level. I find people often have this response when they learn their Profile. So simple. So powerful.

The first thing that rang true for me when I learned about the 6/2 Profile is that Line 6 has three phases (you'll read more about the 6/2 in Chapter 15). When people have a Line 6 in their Profile, for the first thirty years of their life, they act like a Line 3. Line 3 is all about learning through trial and error. Wow! Those first thirty years of my life were definitely crazy. I joke that I think we need a recovery group for people with a 6 Line Profile. Not a pretty sight. Those were very messy years! Just about every 6th Line person I know will tell you something similar. Those first thirty years are tough. Occasionally I meet at 6 Line person who had fun exploring during those years, but that is the exception.

The second thing about being a 6th Line is that it's called *The Role Model*. People with a 6th Line are the old souls. They have a long view of life and understand things people don't necessarily see. This was always my experience, and it was baffling to me what I knew that others didn't understand. Having this reflection was a relief and a salve. It reinforced the belief that I wasn't crazy. It supported me to trust my inner guidance. Which, interestingly, is one of the gifts the 6th Line brings to humanity. They are the *Role Models* showing the way to the new paradigm. By living as an authentic person, true to themselves and following their inner guidance, they teach others what is possible. No surprise, that is the theme of this book. Clearly, I'm in alignment with my entelechy on this one!

The third thing that validated my experience was the understanding that people with a 6th Line tend to hang on the outskirts rather than jump into the middle of gatherings. They tend to focus on taking in the whole picture, rather than engaging directly (with the exception of those first thirty years). Having this reflection gave me permission to let go of pressure that I should be in the center. It let me relax and enjoy my stepped-back stance.

My Line 2, which is Unconscious (you'll learn all about Line 2 in Chapter 4), helped me understand my propensity towards insecurity. It named what I knew: I had special talent, but I couldn't articulate it. I couldn't just bring it out into the world. It had to be recognized by others and called out.

Even as I write this book, I watch this process. My wife reads a chapter and tells me how great it is. I don't know that. I only know to go into my *hermitage* and write. I can see she has taken in what I've written. I can see it's like she has drunk from a deep well. The way she talks about herself and her Profile is different. She is more engaged in the Profiles. Her curiosity is sparked. She's entered the stream of the transmission.

By her response, this book is already a success. She is touched, moved, and changed. She is drawn more deeply into the mystery and magic the Profiles offer.

I am hoping the same will be true for you. I am hoping that your world will be shifted as you begin to better understand yourself through the Profiles. I am hoping that by understanding your clients through the Profiles, their lives will be altered. Together, we will be one step closer to living our entelechy and transforming the world we so fortunately inhabit.

3

HOW TO USE THIS BOOK

THE PROFILES ARE WAITING FOR YOU

How you approach the Profiles will impact what your experience is with them. The Profiles are alive. They are dynamic. They offer insight into how we can best align to bring forward our gifts.

If you want to get the most out of this book, I invite you to come with an open heart and mind.

As students of Tibetan Buddhism, we were told two stories as metaphors to approach the teachings. First to leave our shoes at the door. This was symbolic of leaving our egoic thinking and our past experiences outside. And the second was to come with a clean, empty teacup. If our teacup was full, there was no room for new knowledge. If our teacup was dirty, the teachings would be tainted. If the teacup had a crack, the teachings would leak out.

Come for tea! Come present. Let yourself fully receive what is offered. Bring your curiosity.

Like Tibetan Buddhism, Human Design is a path of testing what is true for you. It is an opportunity to be in relationship with the teachings and discover new possibilities. Always remember that you are the ultimate authority.

There are three simultaneous tracks you can interface with as you read this book. The first is the download of pragmatic, left-brain material that will introduce you to the fundamentals of the Profiles. This is the linear or horizontal path laid out in the chapters of the book:

• In Chapter 4, you will get an initial introduction to Human Design followed by an in-depth orientation to the Profiles.

• In Chapters 5 – 16, you will learn about each of the 12 Profiles. In these chapters, you'll be introduced to the entelechy (the potential) of each Profile, get the overview of the Profile, discover famous people who have that Profile, find out the gifts and the challenges of each Profile, and get ideas on how to work with each Profile. At the end of these chapters is a meditation for each Profile.

• In Chapter 17, we'll take a deep look at the Profiles.

• In Chapter 18, we'll consider some of the obstacles that arise when using the Profiles.

• In Chapter 19, we'll reflect on the journey.

The second track is experiential, right-brain learning. Here you meet the Profiles as energy. As a transmission (I know, we get a little woo here), you connect with the information they bring in a nonlinear way. In this track, the Profiles are beacons of light. They shine the light of awareness. You must be open and present to access this level of information. You have to allow yourself to feel and be moved by what you're reading.

Here, you allow the information to work you. You can open the book to any page and receive this level of teaching.

We could think of the third track as the *sushumna*, or the central channel. In Human Design, we could possibly call it the Knowing Circuitry. Here, the left-brain information and the right-brain experience come together in a deep knowing. There is no active learning here; rather, there is a stillness that you tap into when you connect to the Profiles.

At this point, I experience my 6/2 profile as if I am sitting inside my Profile. It is a resting place. I do not have to act or be any different than I am. I trust my long view of my Line 6. I honor the Hermit needs of my Line 2.

To write this book, I went through a journey of connecting with each of the Profiles on all three levels. I invite you to discover how you interface with the information. You may be surprised!

This book is designed to be a resource. There is a lot of information here. Using it as a resource, you can simply go to the chapter on the Profile you're working with. Read about the entelechy, the themes, the gifts, and the challenges. Contemplate the famous people who have that Profile. Consider how you might best work with that Profile.

This book is also a journey into the Profiles. If you want to use this book as a way to tap into yourself and the people in your life, take your time and enter into inquiry with each Profile. Have a list of people's Profiles as you read a chapter. Think of them. Feel into their lives. Be curious. Are they living in alignment with their Profile? Are you? How do you respond to their Profile? Do you fight it? Honor it? Resist it?

If you want to experience the full depth of the Profiles, start with your own. Sit in meditation. Sit in stillness. Connect with your Profile. Speak to it. Ask it for guidance. Listen to it. Let it guide you.

As you read this book, be aware of how your Profile is influencing how you come to the information. Trust yourself and the process.

RESOURCES

There are a couple things that you'll need when you're working with Profiles. The first, if you don't already have it, is to get your Human Design chart. You simply need to input an accurate birth time, date, and place to get the Profile. Here is a link to download charts for free: https://clientsandhumandesign.com/free-chart/

The second is an understanding that when you work with Profiles you will ultimately want to incorporate people's Human Design Strategy and Authority. If you are not already familiar with these, you can look at my first book. You can buy it on Amazon, or you can download a digital copy for free here: https://www.clientsandhumandesign.com/free-book. Strategy and Authority are the keys that enable us to use the Profiles at the highest level.

Finally, while I don't discuss this explicitly in this book, if you'd like to work with the Profiles at a deeply energetic level, I encourage you to explore using the Human Design Essential Oils created specifically for the Profiles. To order oils: https://plantpranaoils.com/human-design-oils/. For Human Design Essential Oil protocol booklet for the Profiles: https://robinwinn.com/HDprofiles-essentialoils.

Let's begin, shall we?

INTRODUCTION TO THE PROFILES – AN OVERVIEW

A BRIEF INTRODUCTION TO HUMAN DESIGN

We could, theoretically, delve into the introduction of the Profiles without discussing Human Design. But to strip the Profiles of their context would seriously undermine their potential for transforming people's lives. That would render the Profiles no more than a tool, though still a useful one. But the Profiles are so much more than a tool, and to access their full potency, we must first consider the context of Human Design.

Some of you, undoubtedly, are familiar with Human Design, the story of its inception, and the greater understanding of its purpose. Others of you may be new to the Human Design world or would appreciate a reminder of the big picture. This brief introduction is for you. Otherwise, you can skip the next few paragraphs and go directly to *Introducing the Profiles.*

As I mentioned in Chapter 2, Human Design was downloaded to a Canadian fellow in 1987 who was on retreat off the Coast of Spain. When Ra Uru Hu, returned to his room, it was filled with light *beings*. These light *beings* meticulously downloaded the Human Design system over several days. Human

Design is a synthesis of astrology, the Chinese I Ching, the Hindu chakra system, the Judaic Kabbalah, and quantum physics.

The light *beings* explained that Human Design was brought at this time for the evolution of humanity. It was for everyone but particularly for parents to help them parent their children. The understanding is that we are each like a piece of the giant puzzle of humanity. Each one of us is perfectly designed. Each one of us is an integral part of the whole. There is no hierarchy. The question is, are we living our design? Are we aligned with who we are here to be? Are we shining the light that only we can bring? If not – if we are trying to live someone else's puzzle piece – we suffer, and humanity loses out. This turn toward honoring and living as our unique selves is a radical departure from the tribal decree that demands that we honor the needs of the tribe over our own individual call. Human Design, then, is the radical call to be yourself at the highest level.

The basis of the Human Design chart is an accurate birth time, date, and place. This information locates a person in relation to the neutrino stream, the planets, and the 64 Hexagrams of the I Ching. Let me explain:

In traditional astrology, at the time of your birth, the planets were in a particular configuration in the sky. Depending on their location, they were situated somewhere in the 12 astrological houses and in the 12 signs. My wife was born in late March, so her Sun was in the sign of Aries at the time of her birth. She was born early in the morning, before sunrise, so her Sun was in the 12th House. In Human Design, the planets at the time of her birth were in the same place in the sky, but instead of dispersed throughout the 12 houses and 12 signs, they are placed within the 64 Hexagrams of the I Ching. So, for example, the Sun at the time of her birth was in the 17th Hexagram. Her Moon in Western Astrology is located in the 1st House in Taurus. In Human Design, her Moon is in the 8th Hexagram. When you look at her Human Design Chart, you'll see the symbol of the Sun with the number 17.6 next to it and a symbol of the Moon with the number 8.1 next to it.

Just to get a little more complicated as we lay out this foundation, let me explain the .6 that follows the 17, and the .1 that follows the 8 in her chart. We're talking about the I Ching Hexagrams here. A hexagram is six lines counting from the bottom to the top (see Chart #4). Not only is Yarrow's Sun in the 17th Hexagram, it's also in the 6th Line of that 17th Hexagram. Her Moon is in the 8th Hexagram and the 1st Line. Understanding that second number based on the six lines is crucial to understanding the Profiles, and we'll dive into those six lines shortly. But first, let's look at the quantum physics influence in Human Design.

The neutrino stream is made up of tiny subatomic particles that travel close to the speed of light. They have no electrical charge and very little mass. Trillions of them are streaming through our bodies and the universe day and night. Scientists say that neutrinos may be the reason that matter exists. So, how does the neutrino stream fit into this Human Design picture?

At the time of our birth, the neutrino stream picks up the energy of the planets in the Hexagrams. This gives our body its unique substance. In Human Design, we take the combination of the neutrino stream from the moment of our birth and combine it with the neutrino stream at a particular moment three months prior to our birth to create the bodygraph. We call the energies from our actual birth time Conscious and the energies from three months prior Unconscious. If you look at a bodygraph, you will see the Conscious denoted with the color black and the Unconscious with red. When we combine the Conscious and Unconscious neutrino streams, which have picked up the energies of the planets, we have our quantum multidimensional bodygraph. It is our unique puzzle piece.

This puzzle piece is our Human Design blueprint. From it we

can gather an extraordinary amount of information. We can discover things like:

• What's your best strategy to navigate life?

• How do you best function?

• How do you best learn?

• What is your purpose?

• How can you use your energy wisely?

• What drives you?

• What is your spiritual path?

The bodygraph also shows your strengths and vulnerabilities. All, of course, in the context of understanding that your chart, your bodygraph is perfect. No one chart or bodygraph is better than another. All of the puzzle pieces are needed.

When looking at a chart, there are several vantages to enter and access the bounty of the information available. Each piece of the chart brings a slightly different perspective. Together they create a deep understanding and reflection of the person as a whole. Here are some of the aspects to consider when looking at the chart:

• Type and Strategy

• Authority

• The Profiles

- The Centers (Defined/Open)

- Gates

- Channels

- Planets

- Circuitry

- Definition and Splits

- Incarnation Cross

- Life Cycles

You can see there are many layers to take into account. In this book, we are looking at the chart through the lens of the Profiles. However, because Type, Strategy, and Authority are foundational to all aspects of the chart, I've included a brief summary of them at the end of this chapter. Following your Type, Strategy, and Authority enables you to activate and utilize the Profiles at the highest level.

INTRODUCING THE PROFILES

Having the larger context, we can now turn the dial to focus on the Profiles themselves. As I mentioned earlier, the Profiles give us information about our learning styles and how we interact with the world. They give us clarity as we evolve into our potential. They offer pragmatic support on our journey.

In this chapter, we'll look at the nuts and bolts of the Profiles. This is the foundational, left-brain information we need as a ground before diving deeper into the relational and working aspects of the Profiles. Here, you'll learn how the Profiles are determined, the names and meaning of the 6 Lines and the 12 Profiles, as well as how the Profiles and lines are delineated into groups.

HOW TO DETERMINE THE PROFILE

There are two ways to determine the Profile. The first is to merely look at the information that comes with the graph. It will indicate the Profile, followed by two numbers with a slash between them, for instance 2/4. Or the information might simply say, for example, 2/4 Generator. Those two numbers are the Profile.

Type: **Pure Generator**

Profile: **2/4 - Hermit / Opportunist**

Definition: **Single**

Inner Authority: **Sacral**

Strategy: **Respond**

Incarnation Cross: **RAX Penetration 2**

Chart #1

The second way is to look at the graph itself. When you run the bodygraph, you will see two vertical columns with symbols of the planets followed by numbers. The column on the right represents the planets in the Hexagrams at the time of your birth. We call these the Conscious aspect. The numbers of the Hexagram will be in black. The column on the left represents the planets in the Hexagrams roughly three months prior to birth. They will be in red and represent the Unconscious aspect of the chart. The top of each of those columns has the symbol of the Sun followed by a number with a decimal point and another number between 1 and 6.

For example, in Marianne Williamson's chart (Chart #2), the black column (Conscious aspect) has the number 53.2 on the top line following the symbol of the Sun. The number following the decimal point is the first number of the Profile. Remember, it will be a number between 1 and 6. These refer to the 6 Lines of the Hexagram. In this case, the number is 2, so the Conscious Profile is 2. (We'll get to the meaning of those numbers shortly.)

Marianne Williamson

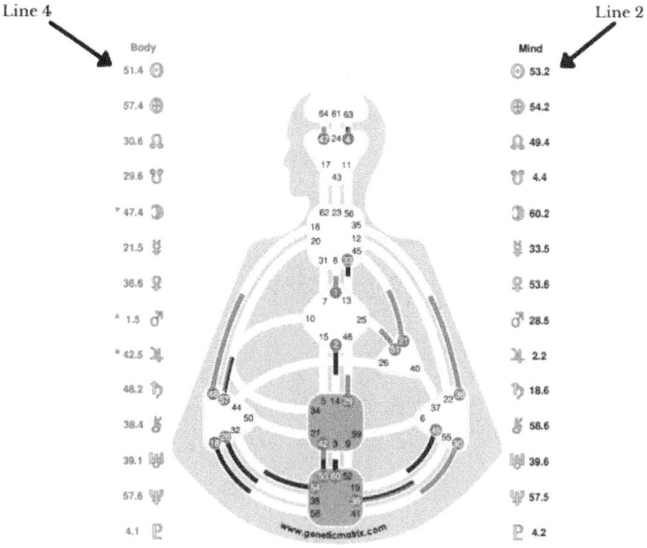
Line 4
Line 2
Body
Mind
www.geneticmatrix.com

Chart #2

Next, turn and look at the second column on the left, which is red (the Unconscious aspect). The top number next to the symbol of the Sun is 51.4. So, the number following the decimal is 4. Thus, the Unconscious Profile is 4. The complete Profile for Marianne's chart is 2/4. The Conscious aspect always comes first; the Unconscious is second.

Take a moment now to look at the next chart (Chart #3). This is the chart of my book mentor and business coach Angela Lauria. Can you tell what she is? Yep, 3/5. In a later chapter, I'll share a bit about her story and what it means to have a 3/5 Profile so you can grok the power of this learning style and the difference between a 2/4 and a 3/5 Profile.

3/5 Profile
Angela Lauria

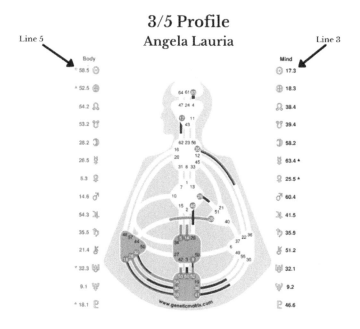

Line 5

Line 3

Chart #3

31

Now that we're clear that the Profile is determined by the lines of the gates in the Conscious and Unconscious Sun signs, let's back up and look at the 6 Lines themselves. What are they? What do they mean?

THE 6 LINES OF THE HEXAGRAM

When we look at the 6 Lines of the Hexagram (Chart # 4), we see that Line 1 starts at the bottom of the chart, and we work up from there.

Line 6

Line 5

Line 4

Line 3

Line 2

Line 1

Chart #4

Next let's look more closely at the 6 Lines with their names and how they're differentiated. You'll notice in Chart #5 that there is a break between the first three lines and the second three lines.

Interpersonal: Self to Others
Line 4 to Line 6

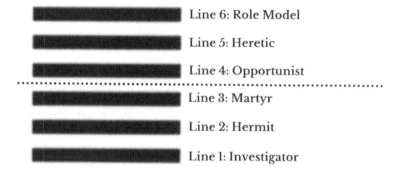

Line 6: Role Model

Line 5: Heretic

Line 4: Opportunist

Line 3: Martyr

Line 2: Hermit

Line 1: Investigator

Intrapersonal: Self to Self
Line 1 to Line 3

Chart #5

The first three lines (again, coming from the bottom up) have a learning style connected to themselves. This is a self-to-self or intrapersonal style. So, if you or someone you're working with has a 1st, 2nd, or 3rd Line Profile (Conscious or Unconscious), you're discovering life and relating what you're learning to yourself.

On the other hand, if you or someone you're working with has a 4th Line, 5th Line, or 6th Line Profile (Conscious or Unconscious), your learning style is interpersonal. You learn about life in relation to others.

As we introduce the 12 Profiles, you will see that the majority of the Profiles have some combination of an intrapersonal and interpersonal learning style. That will be an important part of the conversation as we go forward. These lines are in conversation with one another between the upper trigram and the lower trigram, as well as between the Conscious and Unconscious.

For now, let's come back to those 6 Lines and their meanings.

THE ORIGINAL HUMAN DESIGN NAMES

Heads up: a few of the original Human Design names, honestly, have a somewhat unfriendly vibe. Especially Line 3, 4, and 5. Most people I introduce to Human Design are a bit put off by them. They go into resistance. Who wants to identify with names like Martyr, Opportunist, or Heretic? Really? Nonetheless, when you understand them, they do make a sort of sense.

For example, the 5th Line, the Heretic, is bringing new solutions that break with the norm. People project negatively on what they can't understand. Think of Galileo, who had a 5th Line, The Heretic, and was brought before the Roman Inquisition to defend the theory that the sun, not the earth, was the center of the universe. His views were seen as heretical. He risked prison to bring a new worldview.

The 4th Line is called the Opportunist in Human Design. This person is looking for the opportunities that their community provides. In fact, they are dependent on those opportunities to thrive. It is good and natural for them to look for and take advantage of opportunities. Marianne Williamson needed the support of her 4th Line Opportunist as she ran for president in 2020. She needed resources and connections from her community to get as far as she did in the process.

The 3rd Line is called the Martyr in Human Design. This person willingly sacrifices herself/himself by throwing themselves into situations that may or may not work. They do this as an evolutionary offering, committed to finding a better way. Galileo also had a 3rd Line. Knowing that what he discovered could defy the status quo, he was willing to sacrifice himself to discover the truth.

Over the years as people have connected to the transmission of Human Design they have derived different names for the energies in the chart to evolve the language. I invite you to acknowledge the dodgy aspect of the original Human Design names, and explain the intent of the lines to your clients. I tend to simply speak to the energy of the Line or Profile. That said, when I tune into the energy of the 3rd, 4th, and 5th Lines, names arise that offer a different vibrational frequency. Perhaps ones that people can resonate with and lean into. I offer them here for you to explore for yourself and with your clients.

• Line 3, The Martyr, can also be considered The Experimenter or perhaps The Transformer. This is the energy of learning through experimentation. The intent is to know what works and what doesn't work. The intent is to transform or upgrade through experimentation.

• Line 4, The Opportunist, can also be considered The Connector or The Networker. They are relationally connecting to create opportunities for themselves and others. They enter a web then are supported by and influence that web.

• Line 5, The Heretic, can also be considered The Illuminator, or The Crazy Wisdom Guide. They are bringing a new light to see solutions to problems that were previously unavailable – hidden in the dark. When the light turns on, it is not personal, everyone is able to see. Now if people's eyes are closed…if they are holding on to their ignorance, they will not have access to the new light. They will judge the new solutions which appear heretical or crazy to the norm.

THE NAMES AND MEANING OF EACH OF THE 6 LINES

6 Lines

1
Investigator

2
Hermit

3
Martyr (Experimenter)

4
Opportunist (Connector)

5
Heretic (Illuminator)

6
Role Model

Chart #6

LINE 1

The Investigator

Themes

• Voracious appetite for information

• Engaged in the study of life

• Insecurity – get safety and ground through gathering information

• Need details to understand the big picture

• Their genius is awakened as they stabilize on knowledge and become an authority

Entelechy: *To provide a solid foundation through investigation.*

Line 1 is a bit insecure. It gathers information to find its footing. These are the researchers. These are the great students, forever acquiring information to make sense of life. People with Line 1 *have to* know all they can about whatever they're focused on. They are studying life to discover how it works. When I give a Human Design session to someone with a Line 1 in their Profile, I am sure to cover all the details. That puts their Line 1 at ease. It's healthy for them to immerse themselves in learning all they can. Through their attraction to and absorption in knowledge, they gain security. Ultimately, they can become a stabilizing force for others as they offer their vast wealth of resources. People with a Line 1 in their Profile are creating a stable foundation. Albert Einstein had Conscious Line 1 Profile. Through his research, he created a new foundation for physics.

LINE 2

The Hermit

Themes

• Need their down time away from people

• Insecure

• Unique, natural inborn genius

• Talent is recognized and called out

• Self-contained – don't like interference

Entelechy: To allow their natural genius to emerge, be seen, and come to fruition.

Like Line 1, Line 2 is also insecure. Called The Hermit for good reason, it likes its time away from people. As the Line 2 putzes in their own world, doing what they love, other people see them and call them out. Their innate talent is recognized as something extraordinary. And while people with Line 2 may have a sense of a special gift, they are often not sure how to explain what they do or how they do it. The 2nd Line needs downtime, free of pressure. They wait for a call that will give them the opening to share their treasures, which often lay hidden beneath the surface. If they do not have access to the unimpeded downtime, or if they do not respond to calls in alignment with their blueprint (Type, Strategy, and Authority), they can feel unfulfilled and suffer.

LINE 3

The Martyr (The Experimenter)

Themes

• Learns by trial and error

• Must embody things to know if they work

• Learns through experience

• Bonds made and broken

• Catalysts of change

Entelechy: To determine the next level of possibility on the material plane through experience and experimentation.

The Line 3 Profile is engaged in a full-on dialogue with the material plane. They are challenging the status quo and anything in their path to see if it is correct or if there is a way to improve it. Ra explains that "the keynote of Martyr refers to the 3rd Line's ability to stand up and say, 'This is not true,' and take the heat for it." Perpetual learners as they engage in life, they should never be criticized, but instead asked, *What did you learn?* They may not be the easiest people to be in relationship with as they are always feeling what is off and needing to improve it. Without the Line 3 energy, the world would be woefully lacking. We need the Line 3's resilient and robust capacity to meet life, challenge it, and upgrade it!

LINE 4

The Opportunist (The Connector)

Themes

- Harmonic with Line 1 but interpersonal

- Foundation of the interpersonal lines

- Here to investigate relationships

- Here to impact people they know

- Insecurity around change

- Deeply influential

- Friendly nature

- Ultimate networker

Entelechy: *To enrich communities with their ideas and to transform people's lives through their insight.*

Line 4 is the first of the interpersonal lines. The Line 4 and the Line 1 are harmonic. While the Line 1 is investigating and gathering information about the material world, the 4th Line is gathering information about relationships. Like the 1st Line, there is a quality of insecurity. Line 4 tends to be averse to limbo. Change can be unsettling for them. When there is a change, they prefer to have the next step in place before making the change. For example, they like to have the next house secured before moving out of the one they're in. If they are unhappy in a relationship, they may not leave their current relationship until they have the next relationship in place. The same can be true with jobs.

Deeply relational, the 4th Lines have a friendliness about them that draws people to them. The ultimate networkers, they flourish when they are in the correct network. The right jobs, the aligned relationships, and their ideal homes all come from their network. They have a unique capacity to impact people on a personal level. I think of them as the whisperers. They touch people's lives by the words they speak.

LINE 5

The Heretic (The Illuminator)

Themes

- Highest Line — universalizes their message

- Harmonic with Line 2

- Here to save humanity

- Luminary – lighting the world with their new solutions

- Transpersonal

- Projected on positively and negatively

- Here to influence strangers

- Karmic relationships

- Draw people in need of solutions

Entelechy: To take humanity to the next level of possibility by bringing new solutions.

Line 5 is said to be the highest Line of the Hexagram. We would assume it would be the 6th Line, and while the Line 6 does bring a kind of closure, it also is also looking forward to the next Hexagram's 1st Line. We could think of the progression in terms of the maiden/mother/crone archetype. Perhaps the first three lines are like the maiden exploring the world, trying to figure out what life is all about. The 4th Line might be the new mother trying to stabilize the home, dependent on the community for support. The 5th Line could be the mature mother, a problem solver, volunteering or working to save the future of humanity. The 6th Line might be the Crone, the wise guide. She is physically on the decline yet at the height of wisdom. The crone sees the grandchildren ushering in a new cycle.

So, Line 5 takes everything in the chart to a universal level. The energy is transpersonal rather than personal. The light they shine is like the sun, the solutions they bring light up the world. Again, think of Galileo. Line 5 is harmonic with Line 2, which has that quality of being hidden and a seductiveness in that hiding. The 5th Line challenge? People sense that those with a Line 5 can help them and they project on the 5th Line. It's as if the Line 5 is acting as a mirror for people, showing them what they want to see. If the Line 5 can solve the problem at hand, they are heralded as the savior. If they are not able to solve the problem, they fall from grace and are blasted with negative projections. As a result, people with Line 5 can have a shy quality and only show a few people who they really are.

Always in the ready for the next crisis, it's important for the 5th Line Profiles to be in the right place to get the right projections. They must choose wisely the problems they agree to take on and to step out once they have played their part. Otherwise, they risk potent negative projections.

Unlike the Line 4 person, who is here to impact people from their network in an intimate way, the people with Line 5 in their Profile are here to influence strangers. For example, I had never heard of Angela Lauria (3/5 Profile) when I saw her ad to write a book show up on my Facebook feed. She was reaching out to strangers. I watched her webinar and signed up for her program. I saw her as someone who could help me write a book. If her program had not worked for me, I would have undoubtedly blamed her rather than my own limitations.

With this blueprint of impacting strangers of consequence comes an understanding that their relationships are karmic. We could say everyone's relationships are karmic, yet there is something unique for people with 5th and 6th Lines. Every encounter can potentially be life changing either for themselves or for the person they are meeting.

LINE 6

The Role Model

Themes

• Harmonic with Line 3

• Triphasic:

  ○ From birth to thirty, they act like 3rd Lines, learning by trial and error
  ○ From thirty to fifty, they step back and learn by witnessing
  ○ From fifty onward, they become the *Role Model*

• Has the long view – the eagle's view of life

• Can see ahead, and can't understand why others can't see what they see

• Wise souls/old souls

• Stay on the outskirts of a group

• Karmic relationships

• Here to impact strangers of consequence

• Looking for their soulmate

Entelechy: To embody, witness, and live the highest potential of what it means to be human as the Role Model of possibility for others. To claim and live by their inner authority.

Line 6 stands out from the other lines. It is the only line that has three life phases. They have a theme of maturing over time.

• For their first thirty years, the person with a 6th Line in their Profile lives the life of a Line 3. They are bumping into life, discovering firsthand what does and does not work. This is a hands-on, in-the-flesh kind of learning. And while we say the 3rd Line doesn't make mistakes, the experience of these first thirty years can feel like one mistake after another to the Line 6 person.

• Having been bumped around those first thirty years, the 6th Line then shifts gears. From around age thirty to fifty, they step back from the fire of learning by lived experience and become the observer. From this vantage, they gain perspective on life.

They are witnessing what works and what doesn't work. They are building their data base of wisdom and clarity.

• It is with some confidence, then, that around age fifty, things shift. They hit what's called their Kiron return, and for the remainder of their lives, they embody the Role Model. However, to harvest their full capacity to share their *role model* wisdom with the world, they must embrace and integrate what they have learned in the first two phases.

Having navigated these three phases, the Line 6 now can experience life from different vantages. Adding to that depth of experience is a long-view perception – a bird's eye or eagle's view. People with a 6th Line Profile can see what's ahead. They know things that others can't yet see. This can be extremely exasperating for the 6th Line when what is obvious to them is not yet available for others to see.

A Line 6 person is an old soul who is inclined to trust their own inner authority over the authority of others. Living their truth, they become the *Role Models* of this turn toward trusting our unique entelechy. They are modeling the path we are all headed towards. If a Line 6 person has abandoned their inner authority – if they are not living their puzzle piece – they can feel lost and disoriented.

Sometimes seen as aloof, the Line 6 is merely standing back and watching rather than rushing in to be the center of activity. It can be validating and relieving to the 6th Line to realize this is their nature. The alternative is feeling like they should be more involved and making themselves wrong for their distance.

Like the 5th Lines, they are said to have karmic or destiny relationships. Everyone they meet matters in their evolutionary process. And again, like Line 5, they are here to work with and influence strangers. They are here to encounter people previously unknown to them.

Finally, Line 6 has the call to find their soulmate. They are looking for the person who will be their life partner. They may feel incomplete until they find that person.

PUTTING IT ALL TOGETHER: THE 12 PROFILES

You're now familiar with the 6 Lines and their meanings. It's time to take a first look at how those numbers come together.

There are 12 combinations of Profiles. Each combination has two numbers representing the energy of two lines of the Hexagram. Again, the first number is derived by the Conscious Sun. We are typically more aware of this energy. The second number is derived from the Unconscious Sun, and we may or may not be as aware of that energy. It may take some work on our part to recognize, honor, and utilize the Unconscious Profile. Each combination that creates the Profile acts as a synergistic, transformational force both for the individual and for the collective of humanity. To fully embody and live our entelechy and to bring our unique gifts to humanity, we need our Profile to be activated and engaged.

There are three groupings of Profiles divided by what is called the Incarnation Cross. The study of the Incarnation Cross is a whole other book, but for our purposes, all you need to know is that the Incarnation Crosses tell us the nature of a person's destiny. If you look at the chart (see Chart #6), The Right Angle Crosses, which have a personal destiny, are in the left column. The Juxtaposition Cross, which has a fixed fate, is in the middle column. And Left Angle Crosses, which have a transpersonal destiny, are in the right column. This is something to keep in mind as you're working with clients. Look at Chart #7 to see the Profiles grouped by Crosses. Chart #8 shows the names of the Profiles by Crosses.

The 12 Profiles by Crosses

Right Angle Crosses	Juxtaposition Cross	Left Angle Crosses
1/3	4/1	5/1
1/4		5/2
2/4		6/2
2/5		6/3
3/5		
3/6		
4/6		

Chart #7

THE 12 PROFILES

Right Angle Crosses

1/3: Investigator/Martyr

1/4: Investigator/Opportunist

2/4: Hermit/Opportunist

2/5: Hermit/Heretic

3/5: Martyr/Heretic

3/6: Martyr/Role Model

4/6: Opportunist/Role Model

Juxtaposition Cross

4/1: Opportunist/Investigator

Left Angle Crosses

5/1: Heretic/Investigator

5/2: Heretic/Hermit

6/2: Role Model/Hermit

6/3: Role Model/Martyr

Chart #8

STRATEGY AND AUTHORITY

The key to aligning with your Profile is to follow your Strategy and Authority. These are the foundational pieces of Human Design that keep you on track with yourself. Their importance cannot be underestimated. As you align with your Strategy and Authority, your Profile supports your life journey. For the purposes of this book, I'm including a brief review. To understand these more deeply, please read my first book, *Understanding Your Clients through Human Design: The Breakthrough Technology*. https://www.clientsandhumandesign.com/free-book

Strategy

Our Strategy shows us the best way for us to interact with the external world. It is key to optimizing our energy. Knowing your Strategy supports how you work with your Profile. There are five Human Design Types. Each Type has a unique Strategy:

• The Generator Strategy is to respond.

• The Manifesting Generator Strategy is to respond (Generator) and inform (Manifestor).

• The Manifestor Strategy is to inform.

• The Projector Strategy is to wait for the invitation or to be recognized.

• The Reflector Strategy is to wait twenty-nine days before acting or making decisions.

Authority

Authority shows you how to best make decisions given your design. Your chart will indicate your Authority. The following are the different Authorities:

• Emotional Authority: Designed to wait out their emotional wave before making decisions.

• Sacral Authority: Designed to make decisions in the moment in response. (*Ah huh/ah un*)

• Splenic Authority: Designed to make decisions with your intuition and inner knowing. Requires deep listening.

• Ego Manifested Authority: Your voice is your authority. Listen to what you say to know what to do.

• Ego-Projected Authority: Wait to be recognized and invited.

• Mental Authority/No Authority: Speak to a neutral listener to hear yourself.

• Lunar Authority: Take a month before making a decision.

In this chapter, we began the exploration into the Profiles by looking at the big picture. We gave the context of the Profiles within the Human Design paradigm. We introduced the Profiles, including how to determine the Profiles, and we delineated the Conscious and Unconscious aspects of the Profile. We looked at the 6 Lines of the Hexagram, the meaning of each of those lines, and how the 6 Lines combine to make the 12 Profiles. Finally, we gave a brief review of Strategy and Authority. This is the key to living aligned with your Profile. Now we're ready to take the dive into each of the Profiles.

5

THE 1/3 PROFILE

INVESTIGATOR/MARTYR

Themes

• Only Profile with both lines in the lower trigram

• Need information to feel secure enough to explore

• Trial and error approach to discover what does or doesn't work

• Independent

• Focused on Self

• Gather information, then become the authority

Entelechy: The 1/3's passion for research and willingness to discover through exploration ignites a mutative process that ultimately brings an evolving foundational ground to humanity.

Famous 1/3 Profiles

Beyoncé, Princess Diana, Prince Harry, Edgar Cayce, Harry Houdini, Ram Dass, Vincent Van Gogh, Swami Yogananda, Ernest Hemingway, Hillary Clinton, Kate Hudson, Michelle Pfeiffer, Alice Walker, Stacy Abrams, Tracy Chapman, Norah Jones, Celine Dion, Jesse Jackson, Amanda Gorman

Overview

The 1/3 Profile is the only profile where both lines are in the lower half of the trigram. They learn through their personal experience of themselves in relation to the world. With their Conscious Line 1, there is an initial insecurity as they are seeking information to create stability. Navigating survival issues, they look to establish a secure foundation. As they gather the needed knowledge, they have enough safety and ground to step out and explore the world with their trial-and-error process. Continuously seeking what works, their Unconscious Line 3 encounters the material world, discovering in a very hands-on way what doesn't work. With this knowledge, they recalibrate again and again to align more closely with what does work. Thus, they embody a mutative energy that brings a new level of possibility for humanity.

THE CONSCIOUS LINE 1

The Investigator

The Conscious Line 1 is providing a solid foundation through investigation. Fundamentally insecure, they are driven to gather information. As they research, they gain confidence. They look to those who have a higher degree of knowledge to inform them. The more the Line 1 knows, and the better educated they are, the more secure they feel. Self-absorbed, they are intent on understanding how life works. They can spend hours in their own world, deep in concentration. Someone with a Conscious Line 1 will readily acknowledge their need for information.

When I give a Human Design session to someone with a Line 1 Profile, I am sure to cover all the details of the chart. That puts the Line 1 at ease. The 1st Line can feel uncomfortable until they have mastered what they need to know. Through their attraction to and absorption of knowledge, they gain security. Ultimately, they become a stabilizing force for others as they offer the bounty of what they've discovered.

THE UNCONSCIOUS LINE 3

The Martyr (The Experimenter)

The Unconscious Line 3 is here to determine the next level of possibility on the material plane. Doing this requires trying things on in a lived way to see what does and doesn't work. They then share their discoveries with the world.

Because the Line 3 is Unconscious they may not readily acknowledge their 3rd Line. Nonetheless, they are at their best when they are fully engaged with the material plane. Challenging the status quo and anything in their path, their dharma is to test life. In this way, they can see if the information is correct or if there is a way to improve it. Perpetual learners, they engage in life in a robust and wholehearted way. They are designed to meet life, challenge it, and upgrade it!

In relationships, there can be a bonds-made-and-broken theme. If something is not working in a relationship, they feel it and, naturally, want to upgrade it. They may pull away to do more research, coming back to find a new way of relating. Or there may not be a viable new way, and the relationship falls away, making space for the next experience.

THE 1/3 PROFILE

With the 1/3 Profile, we are combining two very different energies. In Line 1, we have the researcher. They are trying to make sense of life through their mind and the material world. In Line 3 we have the discoverer who must experience something in an embodied way order to know if it's true or not.

If the Line 1 research is stifled, the 1/3 Profile can suffer a debilitating insecurity. Without the research, they lack the safety that enables them to do the experimenting that gives them the truth they are seeking. However, when they can do the research that creates safety, they have an extraordinary capacity to interact with life in a creative and mutative way. The 1/3 Profile discovers what works and what doesn't by learning from their so-called "mistakes." They then integrate what they've learned. This gives them a potential resilience to transform any situation to the next level of coherence.

Self-oriented and independent, the 1/3 Profile learns from authorities on their path. When they are in alignment with their Profile, they then become the authority. This Profile tends to move forward in life in a measured way, taking risks when it is safe to do so.

The 1/3 Profile is the first of the seven Right Angle Crosses. Thus, it has a Personal Destiny. People with a 1/3 Profile are here to explore their personal experience of life rather than exploring other people's processes. Their Type, Strategy, and Authority will determine how they best interact with the world given their Profile.

Gifts

The 1/3 Profile brings a particular gift to humanity. Their minds are amazing. With an insatiable appetite for knowledge, their inquisitive curiosity gathers and stores information. Like true researchers, they then test what they've learned to see if it in fact holds up in real life. We rely on people with 1/3 Profiles to continuously evolve our world to higher and higher levels through their willingness to "make mistakes" in the service of discovering what works.

As a 1/3, Lee Glickstein is the founder of Speaking Circles International and originator of the term *Relational Presence*. After a lifetime of stage fright, he discovered a radical and effective approach to public speaking. Through his research and experimentation, Lee became an international authority on authentic power and presence in public speaking. He is continuously developing and refining the work of speaking from presence.

Nina Sossamon-Pogue is another 1/3 Profile. She is a keynote speaker on Resiliency, Adversity, and Achievement. Nina combines data, psychology, and experiential learning to help people navigate life challenges. Her moving personal story is chronicled in her book, *This Is Not the End: Strategies to Get You Through the Worst Chapters of Your Life*. Here, Nina demonstrates the path of the 1/3 as she made the national USA Gymnastics team and was an Olympic gold medal hopeful only to "mess up" in the final trials. Story after story, you watch her rise and (what looks like) fall. Only each time, she learns valuable lessons, which catapult her to the next level of her journey. Researching the neuroscience of resilience, combined with her own lived experience, Nina is the expert who now helps others to embrace their "downfalls" and find new meaning as they integrate the learning into their lives and go forth renewed.

Challenges

There are a few challenges the 1/3 Profile can face.

For one, they can get stuck in the Line 1 aspect – the insecurity. If they cannot get the information, they need to feel safe enough to venture out into the land of experimentation, they can freeze. Picture the spinning ball of the computer trying to find the files but not able to access them. This can be quite debilitating. It can keep the 1/3 from realizing the 3rd Line exploratory aspect of their Profile.

On the other hand, if they jump into the 3rd Line exploration without having first done their research, they can find themselves in situations that leave them reeling, unable to assimilate their lived experience and their exploration in a productive way. I remember the time my dad came home from the hospital with a long face. He had just been in the emergency room with a young man who dove headfirst into a lake, hit his head, and was now paralyzed. He hadn't checked out the depth of the water before diving.

Research is fundamental to the well-being of the 1/3. If they do not have access to an education, it hinders their capacity to gain the knowledge they need to step into their role as the authority. This can leave them feeling inadequate, and without a foundation to explore the world.

Finally, because the 1/3 Profile is designed to learn and navigate life through their personal, lived experience, they can be perceived as selfish or self-centered. There is some truth to this and is as it should be. They rely on their self-orientation to give them the information they need before they can offer what they've discovered to others.

WORKING WITH A 1/3 PROFILE

When you are working with a 1/3 profile, you want to consider their independent nature, their need for information, a drive for security, and a spirit of learning by fire. You will want to support them to take their time researching all the data until they are satisfied, until they feel safe enough to leap into the world of experimentation. Help them to understand that their trial-and-error nature should never be viewed through the lens of "mistakes." Rather, the question becomes, *What did you learn?* And instead of hiding in shame, support them to integrate their learning in preparation for the next experiment.

Think of the process of making rockets. How often did the first rockets fail? Each failure led to a recalibration. If the scientists couldn't tolerate the failures, we would have no rockets or airplanes or cars or electricity or laparoscopic surgeries...

This is the nature of the 1/3. They try. They learn from what didn't work. They try again.

Celebrate this process with your client! Encourage them to embrace both aspects of their Profile. Help them to reframe past experiences where they may have been blamed, or blamed themselves, for trying things that didn't work out.

Sometimes, you may have a client who is spinning in the Line 1 world, unable to get enough knowledge to feel safe enough to step out and explore. Or perhaps they're caught in a belief that they've made a mistake, and this has hijacked their natural inclination to explore. It could be that the understanding of their Profile can give them the perspective they need to unhitch from the story of failure or inadequacy. When that is not enough, you may need to work with them to support their research or to help them navigate their beliefs around making mistakes.

GUIDED MEDITATION

Imagine for a moment that you are a once-in-a-lifetime, unique *being* brought to Earth with a special mission. You have an important purpose. What you're here to bring is an invaluable piece contributing to the larger puzzle of humanity. Your light cannot be replicated by anyone else.

To ignite your purpose and ensure that your light is turned on, you've been given a gift, your Profile. You have been gifted the 1/3 Profile. This Profile gives you insight into how to realize your potential. It shows you the mechanism or the learning style that will call forth your purpose.

> *Take a moment to connect with your 1/3 Profile.*
> *Put everything aside.*
> *Let the past fall away.*
> *Let the future dissolve.*
> *Turn your attention to the present moment.*
> *Allow your awareness to shift from ordinary consciousness*
>   *to extraordinary consciousness.*
> *Begin to settle into your body.*
> *Sense your arms and legs.*
> *Sense your hands and feet. Breathe.*
> *Relax.*
> *Open.*
> *Allow yourself to be here now.*
> *Let yourself occupy your place on earth.*
> *Now imagine that you came to planet earth with a*
>   *purpose.*
> *You are unique, brilliant, and magnificent.*
> *Sense your breath as you allow yourself to rest into your*
>   *being.*
> *You have a mission, and a specific way to bring your*
>   *mission to fruition.*

You have a 1/3 Profile.

*Your superpower is using your drive for information to
    gather as much knowledge as you can until you know
    it's safe to step out.*

Feel the ground of your knowledge.

The power and safety it brings.

But it is not enough.

You must test it.

You must find out if it is hearsay or if it is, in fact, truth.

You need to experiment.

You get your hands messy.

Your life gets messy.

*You don't know if something will actually work until you
    try it.*

Some people judge you for trying.

*They can only see what didn't work, as if that was the end
    of the story.*

You know better.

You know that is just the beginning.

*You know that the so-called mistake is as important as any
    success you might experience.*

*You see everything as an approximation on the path to
    mastery.*

Take a breath.

Recognize your path.

Appreciate your independent streak.

Appreciate your curiosity.

*Appreciate your willingness to take risks once you have the
    information you need.*

This is your path.

Allow yourself to embrace it. Welcome it. Celebrate it.

*Take a moment to ask if there is any guidance the 1/3
    ~Profile has for you at this time.*

What, if anything, do you see, hear, or sense?

Imagine yourself going forward with this new under-
standing.
You are ready to rock the world!
Smile at your 1/3 Profile.
Thank it.
And simply taking a breath,
Come back to your body.
Sense your arms and legs.
Allow yourself to be still and integrate your opening.
Now anchor your experience by writing down your
thoughts.
Do you have any takeaways?

Note: If you want an audio recording of this meditation, reach out to me with your Profile details at info@clientsandhumandesign.com.

THE 1/4 PROFILE

INVESTIGATOR/OPPORTUNIST

Themes

- Introspection/connection

- Insecurity/security

- Drive for knowledge to create a foundation then share

- Network is everything

- Here to impact people on a personal level

Entelechy: The 1/4 genius lies in their insatiable curiosity to understand the world coupled with their capacity to share what they discover with humanity.

Famous 1/4 Profiles

Albert Einstein, Albert Camus, Jose Canseco, David Copperfield. Emily Dickenson, Benjamin Franklin, Indra, Nisargadatta Maharaj, Henry Miller, Louis Pasteur, Jerry Seinfeld, Janet Yellen, Gloria Steinem, Jessica Alba

Overview

The 1/4 is brilliant. With a keen curiosity, they cultivate knowledge with the ultimate intent of impacting people within their network. They need to balance their profound need for introspection time with their equally important need to share what they've discovered with the community. Both Line 1 and Line 4 have an inherent insecurity as they are seeking a foundation. As the 1/4 learns from experts and becomes an authority, it shifts its insecure sensibility to a secure one. It shifts from the need to establish a solid foundation to becoming an authority and establishing a foundation in a transpersonal arena. The need for the right network is key for the 1/4 Profile to carry out this life project.

THE CONSCIOUS LINE 1

The Investigator

This Conscious Line 1 has a quality of insecurity. They are driven to research. Intent on understanding the material world, Line 1 finds its ground through information. These are the great students of life. Line 1 has to know all they can about whatever they're focused on. They are compelled to discover how life works. It's healthy for people with Line 1 to immerse themselves in study. As they are attracted to and absorb knowledge, they gain security. As they become experts and share their extensive knowledge, they bring a stability to others. Line 1's insatiable curiosity and drive to understand life brings a foundational ground to humanity.

THE UNCONSCIOUS LINE 4

The Opportunist (The Connector)

Line 4 is the first of the interpersonal lines. The Line 4 typically does not do well with limbo. Change can be unsettling for them. When there is a change, they will handle it better if they have the next step in place before making the change. The gap is not great for them. For example, it's best if they have the next house secured before moving out of the one they're in. If they are unhappy in a relationship, they may not leave their current relationship until they have the next relationship in place. That would be healthy for Line 4. The same is true with jobs. They may find it difficult to find the next job if they leave before they have one in place. Remember, this is unconscious, so it may take some reflection for the 1/4 Profile to recognize their 4th Line influence.

Deeply relational, the Unconscious Line 4 Profile has a need for community and a strong network. You could say that their lives depend on their network. Their jobs, their relationships, and their homes all come from their network. They have a unique capacity to impact people on a personal level through their network.

THE 1/4 PROFILE

Line 1 is harmonic with Line 4. Both Lines are focused on gathering information about the world, but while Line 1 is engrossed in understanding the material world, Line 4 is drawn to understanding relationships. Both lines are foundational: Line 1 is the foundation of the lower trigram, while Line 4 is the foundation of the upper trigram. In their foundational role, they are naturally insecure. Their path is to pacify that fundamental insecurity by gaining knowledge and becoming experts. This gives them a solid ground they then bring to humanity.

When we combine the harmonically tuned Line 1 and Line 4, we have the potential for magnificent impact. We have the combination of introspection (Line 1) and connection (Line 4) on full display. A good example of this is Benjamin Franklin, a leading intellect in his time who is noted on Wikipedia as being "active as a writer, scientist, inventor, statesman, diplomat, printer, publisher and political philosopher." He was a successful newspaper editor and printer in Philadelphia and made his fortune publishing *Poor Richard's Alamanack*, where he shared information and insight throughout the Thirteen Colonies for over twenty-five years. Can you see how this is vintage 1/4 activity? He gathered information, then shared it with the community.

The 1/4 Profile is also one of the seven Right Angle Crosses. Thus, it has a Personal Destiny. People with a 1/4 Profile are here to explore their personal experience of life rather than exploring other people's processes. Following their Type, Strategy, and Authority will ensure they attract the correct network and share the appropriate information in the right timing to transform people's lives.

Gifts

The tremendous gifts the 1/4 brings begins with their compulsion to understand life, to use knowledge to gain mastery. Their Conscious Line 1 has the gift of investigating and mastering knowledge. Their Unconscious Line 4 has the gift of cultivating a network for the purpose of sharing that knowledge. The meeting and harmonizing of those two lines create the conditions and the foundation for people to thrive at a higher level. Think of Albert Einstein in the area of science. Think of

Benjamin Franklin in the area of government. Think of Nisarga-datta in the area of spiritual awakening.

Challenges

The 1/4 Profile needs their lines to be working harmoniously with one another if they are to flourish. The Line 1's need for introspection must be in harmony with the Line 4's need for social contact. Social interaction must be balanced with deep solitude. Only when the 1/4 can share their knowledge to the right people can they realize their gifts.

If the 1/4 does not have their introspection time, they will not be able to do the research they need. Thus, they will not gather the information necessary to establish a foundation. If the introspection is not in place, then the second part of the equation – sharing the information with their network – can't happen.

If the introspection is in place but there is no network, then, as in the previous scenario, the entelechy or the genius of the 1/4 is not realized. The knowledge, brilliant as it may be, has no soil to land in. In the same way, the network must be a healthy one, formed through alignment with the Type and Authority. (See *Understanding Your Clients through Human Design: The Breakthrough Technology*: https://www.clientsandhumandesign.com/free-book.) If it is not a healthy network, then the recipients won't be available for the knowledge the Line 1 is bringing. In this case, it's like a seed planted in the wrong soil.

The 1/4 Profile has a message to bring. If someone doesn't receive their message or challenges it, the 1/4 Profile will not confront or try to convince the person. The 1/4 will simply shift their focus away from those people.

WORKING WITH A 1/4 PROFILE

Being one of the *Harmonic* Profiles, there are fewer people who have the 1/4 Profile. My pool of clients with a 1/4 Profile is limited, but here is what I can say:

You need to stress the importance of their solitary study time engaging in something that fascinates them. That must be in place. Support them to respect and honor that need. This is the backbone of their success. Secondly, you'll need to have the network conversation. Are they in a good network? Do they have a place to share their wisdom and insights? How are they with their timing regarding sharing their insights? Is what they have to say being received? This will tell you if they're following their Strategy and Authority or if you'll need to address that issue.

I have a 1/4 friend and colleague, Vivian DeGuzman, from my writing group who came to me for a Human Design session. Vivian had just written and published her bestseller, *Awaken Your Medical Intuition*. Referred to as the Human MRI, Vivian is a business intuitive and multimodality healer. Her dream is to have a worldwide impact with the information she has mastered regarding money magnetism and health. Vivian aligned with her Human Design awareness as a 1/4 Manifesting Generator and created a strategy that supported her. I've watched her network blossom and her impact expand exponentially as she established her TV show and podcast. She is here to have a broad reach.

Another 1/4 friend and colleague, Natalie Wall Pereman, also in my writing group, came for a Human Design session. She wrote the bestselling book *The Mom's Guide to Thrive after Loss, Trauma and Abuse*. As a 1/4 Projector, her path to creating a community in order to share her wisdom was different than Vivian's. In the course of a year, Natalie established a Facebook group named *Witchy Moms* that has over 36,000 members, and her Instagram has 40,000 followers. She shares daily wisdom, like today's message:

"Once you stop accepting breadcrumbs the Universe will know to send you the whole slice."

— AUTHOR UNKNOWN

I can assure you, this is aligned 1/4 activity.

GUIDED MEDITATION

Imagine for a moment that you are a unique, once-in-a-lifetime being brought to Earth with a special mission. You have an important purpose. What you are here to bring is invaluable to the larger puzzle of humanity. Your light cannot be replicated by anyone else.

To ignite your purpose and ensure that your light is turned on, you've been given a gift, your Profile. You have been gifted the 1/4 Profile. This Profile gives you insight into how to realize your potential. It shows you the mechanism or the learning style that will call forth your purpose.

Take a moment to let go of the past and rest in the present moment.

Allow your awareness to shift from ordinary consciousness to extraordinary consciousness.

You are turning on the light of awareness to explore your 1/4 Profile.

Begin by sensing your arms and legs.

Let yourself arrive in your body.

Take a breath into your belly center.

Gently stretch to find a comfortable resting place.

Now, open to the Conscious Line 1 of your Profile.

Recognize yourself as someone who is nourished by information.

See yourself immersed in studying something that delights you.

See something that fascinates you and that inspires you.

Appreciate the sensation of having your cup filled as you gain knowledge that excites you.

Now, feel the urge to share that knowledge.

Look around.

Who is your tribe?

Your people?

Who is waiting to hear what you have discovered?

Feel the desire to take this knowledge to a larger field.

Imagine writing your thoughts or speaking your awareness.

Imagine people reading your words or listening to your voice.

Notice how people's lives are transformed by your offering.

Now, watch as your words continue to move through your network.

Alive. Powerful. Dynamic. Transformative.

Is this you?

Are you aligned with yourself? Do you have the time you need to be introspective?

Do you have the community in place, at the ready to hear your wisdom?

Or do you need to make a shift to allow more of you to come forth?

Regardless of where you are on your journey, decide to align more closely with yourself.

Take a moment to appreciate this gift you have:

The gift of curiosity and wonder.

The capacity to share your wisdom.

Smile at your 1/4 Profile.

Ask it if there is any information your Profile has for you.
Thank it.
And when you're ready, gently bring your awareness back
*   to your body.*
Sense your arms and legs.
Sense your belly center.
Take a breath.
And slowly bring your awareness back into the room.
Take a moment to journal and anchor your experience.
What did you discover?
Can you put it in words?

Note: If you want an audio recording of this meditation, reach out to
me with your Profile details at info@clientsandhumandesign.com.

7

THE 2/4 PROFILE

HERMIT/OPPORTUNIST

Themes

- Shy and bold

- Need to balance *hermit* time with social time

- Innate gifts are seen and called out when *hermitting*

- Network is key to success

- Here to impact people on a personal level

Entelechy: The 2/4 Profile has the enviable capacity to connect with their innate talents then share them with the world in the right time and place. In this way they bless and transform the world.

Famous 2/4 Profiles

Simone Biles, Barbra Streisand, Elon Musk, Oprah Winfrey, Marianne Williamson, Susan B. Anthony, Kamala Harris, Bill Clinton, Julian Assange, Coleman Barks, Nicholas Cage, Tom Cruise, Johnny Depp, Jeff Bridges, Gerard Depardieu, Bobby Fischer, Jane Fonda, Gwyneth Paltrow, Joyce Carol Oates, Erica Jong, Emily Post, Aretha Franklin, Quincy Jones, Ray Charles, Victor Frankl, Octavio Paz, Carl Jung, John Lennon, Michael Moore, Rudolph Steiner, Osho

Overview

The 2/4 Profile has an unusual and interesting dynamic. They live between the tension of needing time to be by themselves to honor their Hermit and needing time to be with others to engage socially. Their Conscious Line 2 calls them inward, while their Unconscious Line 4 calls them out into the world. They are here to impact the people they know through their network. They also rely on their network to connect them with the resources they need to find ideal relationships, jobs, and homes. Slightly insecure (both the Line 2 and Line 4), they gain security as their gifts are called out and their life purpose is fulfilled.

THE CONSCIOUS LINE 2

The Hermit

The Conscious Line 2 is learning by its connection to itself. People with this line need time away from others to be with themselves. As the Line 2 putters uninterrupted in their own world, doing what they love, their gifts are seen by others. Their innate talent is recognized. They have a special capacity that needs no study. They may not be able to articulate their gifts even if they sense them. But as they *hermit*, they wait for a call that will allow them to reveal their unique offering. When they respond to the correct calls, the world is blessed.

THE UNCONSCIOUS LINE 4

The Opportunist (The Connector)

The Unconscious Line 4, on the other hand, is deeply relational. It is the first of the interpersonal lines. In harmonic with the Line 1, which is investigating and gathering information about the material world, Line 4 is gathering information about relationships. This Line is the foundation of the upper trigrams. As such, it has that insecure nature. Change can be problematic for the 4th Line. Transitions can be challenging. Having the next step in place is grounding for them. They will feel more secure if they have established their next place of residence before moving out of the home they're in. These are the people who will start dating someone new before they leave their current partner. They may stay longer in a job than is good for them while they're procuring the next stable employment.

People with a Line 4 Profile are friendly and deeply relational. This open quality draws people to them. When they are following their Strategy and Authority, a network naturally forms around them. Through this network, they are introduced to people who become their partners, they are invited to apply for jobs, and they hear about their next home. With a unique capacity to deeply impact people on a personal level, 4th Line Profiles shift the trajectory of people's lives.

THE 2/4 PROFILE

When the Conscious Line 2 combines with the Unconscious Line 4, a dynamic tension ensues. The Hermit's urge is to be alone, while the Opportunist's urge is to connect. Ideally, the Line 2 gets the *hermit* time it needs to be in their own flow, follow their inner impulses, and discover their innate gifts. While in their own world, they are seen and called out to share their treasures with others. When they respond to the call from a place of alignment with their Type, Strategy, and Authority and are ignited by the invitation from a person in the right network, their world can open up in powerful and deeply impactful ways. Thus, they fulfill their destiny calling.

Think of Marianne Williamson and Oprah Winfrey. Clearly, their Unconscious Line 4 is engaged. They have huge networks and are figureheads in the world. They present as relational, friendly, and available. But how much do you know about Marianne or Oprah's personal lives? Very little. They step out into the public arena but live in their private world. Both have gifts – I say innate gifts – that arise rather than gifts that are the result of perfection through study.

Oprah has the gift of conversation, drawing people out, and following stories that touch and empower people's lives. Marianne has the gift of listening and articulation. I've spent the past year in a small mastermind coaching group led by Marianne. Each week, I watched in awe as she assessed a situation, either someone's personal share or a world event. Most of the time, when she responded, it was as if the clouds parted and the light of truth illuminated the situation, bringing an expanded clarity and spiritual reckoning. You might argue that she has spent the last forty years studying *A Course in Miracles*. True. And, there are many people who have devoted their lives to studying A *Course in Miracles*. Are you hearing about them?

Marianne tells the story of being in her own world in the early nineties, teaching *A Course in Miracles* at churches in Los Angeles, when a friend suggested she make a book from her lectures. What quickly unfolded was the publishing of her first book, *A Return to Love*, which has sold over 1.5 million copies and has been translated into twenty-three languages. Marianne's gift was seen and called out.

If you look at the list of famous people with a 2/4 Profile, first, you will notice how many of them there are. And I didn't include all of them... Look at this list and include the people you know who have a 2/4 Profile. You will see that shy/bold theme playing out. Or you will see that one side of the Profile has hijacked the person (they're not honoring their *hermit* side or they're not allowing their social side).

My father and three of my siblings have a 2/4 Profile, as do many of my friends and clients. I've seen the *hermit* or social aspect of their lives play out in a variety of ways. My brothers live somewhat solitary lives, but at the same time, they have huge networks and followings. Both have spent their lives immersed in spiritual practices yet have flourished in community. My brother Michael lives at the top of a mountain in Asheville yet teaches qigong all over the world. He hosts a yearly international Qigong retreat with teachers from far and wide. My brother Steven lives in the small town of Fairfield, Iowa, the Transcendental Meditation mecca of the world. Through his distinctive process called Healing the Heart of America, he works with an ever-growing group of global participants to untangle the confusion that clouds our minds and covers our hearts.

My sister Heidi had a different experience with her 2/4 Profile. With a very tribal Human Design chart and an early understanding that she had to be the life of the party in order to have value, Heidi fostered her Line 4 aspect. Community became her source of nurturing. After the death of her teenaged child, Heidi turned inward and began her journey of honoring her *hermit*. Through this work, she found the nurturing within and a connection to herself.

Like the 1/3 and the 1/4 Profiles, the 2/4 Profile is part of the group that have a Right Angle Cross. Thus, people with a 2/4 Profile have a Personal Destiny. Their focus is on their internal process.

Gifts

The 2/4 Profile has the enviable gift of an innate talent and the potential to have a network that calls out those gifts. Here to impact people at a very personal level, we count on people with 2/4 Profiles to say something that will transform people's lives, including our own. We just never know when. The 2/4 Profiles tend to have a friendly, relational, approachable demeanor and a huge capacity to interact socially. Once they respond to an aligned call, a force is activated. Their powerful passion and vibrant aliveness can be unstoppable. When they are aligned, their generosity knows no bounds. They care for and are cared for in their communities. They nourish others and are nourished. The geyser of their giving is something to behold. Almost like one of the Seven Wonders of the World.

Challenges

There are numerous potential challenges with this Profile.

Because the 2/4 is continuously balancing their social and *hermit* sides, they can easily burn out if they do not honor the time they need to reconnect to themselves. When this happens, they can shut down and cocoon in a bubble. They become unwilling to listen to any potential calls. Likewise, if they are not taking the time to *hermit*, they limit their chances of their brilliance being seen.

The 2/4 Profile is vulnerable to insecurity. The Line 2 can feel lost, not knowing what their talents are. It takes others to recognize and mirror them before the innate gifts are revealed. If the Line 4 is not in a good network, they will not get the opportunities they need and can feel without ground or support. In this case, they can be in the wrong relationships, jobs, or homes. This is not a good picture. Likewise, if the 2/4 Profile is not following their Type, Strategy, and Authority, they may mistakenly respond to calls that are not in alignment for them.

If the 2/4 gets caught in the *hermit* aspect, they can hide out, but in a disconnected way that doesn't give them access to their wellbeing and, in turn, their genius. Imagine a Manifesting Generator on their own, busy *doing* without being present. Or someone with an Open Root and Spleen Center alone at home but caught up in pressure and anxiety. Or perhaps someone with an Open Head Center who has been conditioned to believe they should be with others. When they find themselves alone, they are caught in a negative spin, despairing and destitute.

They could be like my sister Heidi, who got caught in a Line 4 cycle of continuously turning outwards to the network, abandoning her connection to herself.

There definitely can be some confusion for the 2/4. Are they introverts or extroverts or both? What are they here to do? How do they explain what they do? Again, depending on the rest of the chart, these challenges can be amplified or mitigated.

WORKING WITH A 2/4 PROFILE

For sure, when you're working with a 2/4 client, you want to acknowledge their amazing capacity as well as the challenges they face. You want to instill in them the importance of having a sanctuary and a place of retreat where they will not be intruded on.

At the same time, you'll want to stand in the knowing that they have a unique gift that is waiting to be offered to the world. Let them know that they may not know what it is and that their time connecting with themselves will reveal it through someone's seeing them. In fact, you may be able to see it and reflect it back to them. Often, especially with someone who has spent more time on the planet, they will acknowledge the importance of their alone time. They have learned to honor this necessary aspect of themselves.

You'll want to explain that as important as their alone time is, they are equally in need of social time. Make clear that their network is tantamount to their success in life. If they are not in a good network, you'll want to encourage them to find or establish one. It is through the network of people they know that they will meet the partners and find the jobs, clients, and homes that are a good match for them.

This is not someone whose best strategy would be to market to strangers.

I asked Jennet Burghard, a relational presence coach, co-author of *Present!* and a student in my *Advanced Human Design Certification Training for Professionals,* what her experience was of finding out she had a 2/4 Profile. She came to the training knowing nothing about Human Design and jumped into the deep end. She explained that it was wonderful to have her Hermit reflected. In the Netherlands, there is a name for this *hermit* aspect: *house chicken.* Her parents endearingly called her a house chicken, as she loved playing on her own doing her own thing. After learning about the Hermit, she recognized her need for it.

In terms of the 4th Line, she says that she never thought about herself as a networker. It was almost the air she breathed – it was so normal. She thought of it as luck. She gave the example of starting her own company. She went to a party, and the husband of her friend said, "I hear your started you own company. I love entrepreneurs, and I will be your first client." For several years, Jennet did in-service programs and developed learning programs for his company.

This is a perfect example of the Line 4 capacity to network and have their needs easily provided.

Jennet also explained that she was conditioned to believe that in marketing, she should be visible to the whole world.

That never worked for her. Whenever she tried to market, she struggled. In truth, clients just come to her. She would always tell people with a quizzical smile that she's never done marketing. Now, with the Human Design understanding of her Line 4 Profile, it all makes sense to her. People call her and ask her for something. She says that people see value in her that she can hardly formulate in herself.

Her advice to working with someone who has a 2/4 Profile is, "Surrender and trust. Enjoy your *hermit* time." She admits that if she gets stuck, she can become invisible. But then life calls on her.

As you look at your 2/4 clients, be curious about their *hermit*/social time. Are they in balance? Are they enjoying themselves and connecting with themselves as they *hermit*? Do they have a sanctuary where they can be uninterrupted? Be curious about their network. Is it good for them? Are they getting called out? Are they responding to calls that support them to flourish?

Recognize that the natural insecurity that comes with the 2/4 Profile is not a flaw that needs to be overcome. It's like a Jaguar that needs regular checkups and needs to be finely tuned. Then, you can run with it. The 2/4 needs to be in tune with themselves. From there, anything is possible.

GUIDED MEDITATION

Imagine for a moment that you are a unique, once-in-a-lifetime being brought to Earth with a particular mission. You have an important purpose. What you're here to bring is invaluable in the larger puzzle of humanity. Your light cannot be replicated by anyone else.

To ignite your purpose and ensure that your light is turned on, you've been given a gift – your Profile. You have been gifted the 2/4 Profile. This Profile gives you insight into how to realize your potential. It shows you the mechanism or the learning style that will call forth your purpose.

> *Imagine for a moment that you came to earth with a*
>   *special gift.*
> *It is unique to you.*
> *But it is somewhat hidden and elusive to you.*
> *Only when you are alone, connecting to yourself, and*
>   *enjoying yourself is it seen.*
> *When the circumstances are right, your gifts will be*
>   *acknowledged.*
> *At that point, you will be asked to share them with the*
>   *world.*
> *Now, take a moment and connect with your 2/4 Profile.*
> *Allow yourself to shift from ordinary to extraordinary*
>   *consciousness.*
> *Come into the present moment.*
> *Settle into your body.*
> *Sense your arms and legs.*
> *Sense your hands and feet.*
> *Breathe.*
> *Relax.*
> *Letting the past fall away, allow yourself to occupy the*
>   *present moment.*
> *Feel yourself as your physical body.*
> *Then, expand your awareness to fill the room.*
> *Continue expanding until you fill all time and space.*
> *Recognize yourself.*
> *You have a mission here on earth.*
> *You are called to bring your hidden treasures to humanity.*
> *What are they?*
> *Do you know?*
> *Can you sense them?*
> *Would it be OK not to have to articulate them?*

How would it be to let them find their way?

Imagine yourself in a sanctuary – your sanctuary.

Here, you are safe.

Uninterrupted, you are free to follow your bliss in your own time in your own way.

What are you called to do?

Can you see?

Can you feel your urges and your desires?

Feel how good it feels to be in timeless space with yourself.

Now, imagine a friend calls.

You don't want to leave your sanctuary, but they are seeing you.

They want something you have.

You check in and realize you'd actually like to step out.

That would feel good too!

You step into the world of people and connections.

You're appreciated and valued.

You have a talent that serves.

It's fun. It's exciting.

You love sharing your gifts.

And then, you've had enough.

It's time to come back, regenerate, and restore.

Gladly, you settle in your sanctuary.

Back home.

With you.

Take a moment to acknowledge your 2/4 Profile.

This aspect of yourself that calls on you to be both introverted and extroverted.

Ask your 2/4 Profile if it has any wisdom for you at this time.

If it does, receive it. Then, thank your 2/4 Profile.

Smile at your 2/4 Profile.

Gently bring your awareness back to your body.

Sense your arms and legs.

Sense your hands and feet.
Sense your belly center.
Take a breath.
And slowly bring your awareness back into the room.
Take a moment to journal and anchor your experience.
What did you discover? Can you put it in words?

Note: If you want an audio recording of this meditation, reach out to me with your Profile details at info@clientsandhumandesign.com.

8

THE 2/5 PROFILE

HERMIT/HERETIC

Themes

- Shy

- Need time alone

- Can neglect themselves to help others

- Projected on (positively & negatively)

- Here to lead in crisis with practical solutions

- Innate genius: People look to them as someone who can help them

- Here to impact strangers of consequence

Entelechy: The 2/5 Profile has the remarkable potential to bring their genius to the world and solve universal problems with pragmatic solutions.

Famous 2/5 Profiles

Ruth Bader Ginsburg, Steph Curry, Mel Brooks, John Coltrane, Kevin Costner, Mark Twain, Betty Friedan, Judy Garland, Martha Graham, Patty Hearst, Ursula Le Guin, Princess Charlotte of Wales, Shirley Temple, Robin Williams

Overview

With the 2/5 Profile, the Line 2 and Line 5 are harmonic. Both the Conscious Line 2 and the Unconscious Line 5 attract projections from others. However, their response to the projections differs. Line 2 wants to be left alone in their own *hermit* world. They don't perceive the projections. They're fine letting others manage the crises that arise. The Line 5 recognizes the projections but is somewhat cautious regarding them. Nonetheless, with their Line 5's drive to help, they are pulled to fulfill their dharma. They are called to engage with people and bring forth practical solutions.

These are people who can tap into extraordinary gifts and genius when they honor their need to *hermit*.

THE CONSCIOUS LINE 2

The Hermit

In this Profile, the Conscious Line 2 has a deep need to be alone, unimpeded, without intrusions. They are most comfortable in their own world doing what they love. Focused on their own needs, they are happy to let others take care of themselves. As the Line 2 honors their passions and desires, their innate gifts are recognized by others. From their *hermitage*, they are called out. However, the Line 2 may not be thrilled about leaving their sanctuary. Not all calls are good calls for them. If the Line 2 is not in tune with their Strategy and Authority, they may respond to something or someone that is not in their best interest.

THE UNCONSCIOUS LINE 5

The Heretic (The Illuminator)

The Unconscious Line 5 elevates the whole chart to a universal level. This is transpersonal energy committed to serving humanity. As the Heretic, fiercely defying all norms, they have a responsibility to save the world. With their influential power, they bring practical solutions to the problems at hand. Paired with the Line 2, these solutions are revealed while they're in their *hermitage*.

Line 5 Profiles are recognized as people who can help. In this context, they are sought out and called upon for assistance. They also call others to them. Sometimes referred to as seductive, they have a magnetic pull that attracts the people they are to serve. The best strategy for a Line 5 is to help by offering the needed practical guidance then retreat, allowing others to complete what they initiated.

Here to impact strangers of consequence, this is the Profile of someone who has karmic relationships. Every meeting is potentially life changing.

THE 2/5 PROFILE

When the Conscious Line 2 is paired with the Unconscious Line 5, we have a highly unusual person. They have a natural hidden quality and actually need time hiding out on their own to honor their Hermit Line 2. It is in this incubator space that their genius is recognized. At the same time, their dharma is to be called out in a big way. They are here to serve humanity at a potent and transformational level. The 2/5 Profiles only realize their potential when their gifts are utilized.

But there are conundrums all along the way. For one, they live in a projection field. When a 2/5 Profile walks into a room, people inevitably sense their ability to help them. People project onto the 2/5. People want the gifts the 2/5 has to offer. People see possibility, hope, and greatness in the 2/5.

Does the 2/5 want to save the day? Do they want to call on their genius and bring practical solutions to the problem at hand? Yes and no. Maybe. Sometimes, they have to be cajoled. Maybe it's not a good request. Maybe the Line 2 needs more *hermit* time before they respond. But until they find the right call and step out with their solution, the 2/5 is likely going to feel unfulfilled.

And then again, once they do step out to save the day, they have to be mindful of when to step away.

The 2/5 Profiles I know and have worked with have a hidden-in-plain-view quality. They have a magical aura – a sense that they can do special things, extraordinary things. Just look at the list of famous people to get a flavor:

• Ruth Bader Ginsburg was the first Jewish Supreme Court Justice and the second woman to serve. A true Heretic, she tenaciously fought for gender equality and women's rights. Utilizing the legal system, she questioned the dominant norms, instigating new laws that transformed American society.

• Steph Curry revolutionized the game of basketball by inspiring players to master the three-point shot. Think about it: True to his Line 2, he practiced on his own, developing a pragmatic approach to making baskets from distances that were not in the mindset of possibility. He was then called to bring the solution of making more points more efficiently to all of basketball.

• Martha Graham is credited with reshaping American dance.

• Betty Friedan sparked the second wave of American feminism and founded the National Organization for Women, whose aim was to elevate women into full partnership with men in mainstream society.

• Shirley Temple, a child actor in the 1930s, brought hope and optimism to Depression-era America with the solution of forgetting one's troubles by opening one's heart. She was first recognized by a talent scout when she was hiding behind a piano at her dance class.

If a 2/5 Profile can embrace both Lines of their Profile, they can be seen and called out to meet the pressing demand. In this way, they carry out the big work they came to do. They transform the world with their genius.

The 2/5 Profile is also part of the group that have a Right Angle Cross. They have a Personal Destiny. Their Type, Strategy, and Authority will determine how they best interact with the world given their Profile.

Gifts

The gifts the 2/5 brings can be extraordinary. They have that capacity to bring novel, practical solutions that can have far-reaching impact. They can bring hope and possibility to humanity. They can lead with an unwavering tenacity, fiercely defying all norms and breaking through seemingly fixed perceptions and barriers. From their hidden vantage, they have the capacity to be great observers.

The bottom line is that the Line 2 has a hidden genius. When it is seen, called out, and put to work for the benefit of humanity through the Line 5, all things are possible.

Challenges

There are a few challenges here. Many of them are in relation to the projection field. Both the Line 2 and the Line 5 are projected on. That means it can be tough to know who they really are, even for themselves. This Profile has a hidden quality. Neither Lines feel particularly safe in the world. Line 2 is aware of potentially being impinged on and pulled out of their sanctuary. Meanwhile, Line 5 is wary of being seen in a less-than-optimal light.

With the Conscious Line 2, they can sense they have a gift but may not be clear on what it is or what to do with it. Remember, the Line 2 has an element of insecurity. They get security by connecting with and offering their gifts. They need that *hermit* environment where they are not intruded on to access their passions. Here, they can follow their natural inclinations and path of discovery. If they don't realize they need that *hermit* time or are not allowed the time, it can impede their access to themselves. Their creative genius may lie in wait without a chance to see the light of day.

When Line 5 is projected on, they are not seen for who they are but rather for who people want them to be. They act as mirrors, showing people what they need to heal in themselves. If the Line 5 is in the wrong place at the wrong time, getting or responding to the wrong projections, they can be the object of negative projections. This can be brutal for the Line 5, especially if they take the projections personally.

If the Line 5 is getting positive projections but then believes the projections to be personally about them, they can get entwined in believing they *are* the savior rather than the bringers of the solution. This can be a heavy and unrealistic burden.

Also, the Line 5 is designed to bring the solution and then step away. Their job is done. It's time to let others take over. If the Line 5 stays too long, the positive projection can turn negative. Likewise, if the Line 5's solution doesn't work, they can be negatively projected on.

Remember that both lines' needs must be taken into consideration. The Conscious Line 2 has a natural need to be alone. If they don't get that time, it makes it harder for their Unconscious Line 5 to meet the needs of others.

WORKING WITH A 2/5 PROFILE

When you are working with a 2/5 Profile, there are a few things to keep in mind. First, know the potential you are sitting with. Hold the intention of helping your client recognize who they are and what circumstances best support them.

Next, acknowledge that they live in a projection field. Explain the high and low side of the projections that come their way. On the high side, people see that they are someone who can help them. On the low side, if they don't come up with workable solutions, their reputation will suffer. Work with them to use their Strategy and Authority to make sure they are responding to calls to serve that are in alignment for them.

You will also want to acknowledge the internal tension they may feel between wanting to be in their own world in their own domain and the impulse or drive to be seen and called to go out into the world to help others. When this tension is named, there is space to witness it and see it for what it is. Otherwise, it's easy to be at the effect of the tension, caught in its web.

There may be a sense of relief when you support the 2/5 Profile to honor their *hermit* aspect. This need to be alone to access oneself is not generally supported in our culture. Lauren Tancredi, a brilliant 2/5 certified Human Design Consultant and Practitioner (HDC&P), said that learning about her 2/5 profile gave her permission to be a little bit of a wallflower. She always felt she was supposed to show up and be outspoken, which was a stretch for her. Even though she is a Manifesting Generator, with her Line 2, she felt more like a Projector.

Reflecting the Line 5 Savior aspect of the 2/5 also can bring a kind of relief to the 2/5. They recognize that feeling of needing to save the world that they perhaps haven't been able to put words to. Or maybe they have questioned that impulse.

Help them understand that when their work is done, they need to step out of the projection field. This, again, is crucial for their reputation and will protect against burnout.

Finally, introduce the power that comes from waiting. They are designed to wait and discern which call will take their gifts out into the world in way that will fulfill their dharma. If they rush to save the world, feeling compelled to care for people, they will crash and burn. If they hold back from the call, they will feel unfulfilled.

GUIDED MEDITATION

Imagine for a moment that you are a unique, once-in-a-lifetime being brought to Earth with a special mission. You have an important purpose. You are bringing an invaluable piece to the larger puzzle of humanity. Your light cannot be replicated by anyone else.

To ignite your purpose and ensure that your light is turned

on, you've been given a gift, your Profile. You have been gifted the 2/5 Profile. This Profile gives you insight into how to realize your potential. It shows you the mechanism or the learning style that will call forth your purpose.

Take a moment to pause and connect with your 2/5 Profile.
Put everything aside.
Let the past fall away.
Let the future dissolve.
Turn your attention to the present moment.
Allow your awareness to shift from ordinary consciousness to extraordinary consciousness.
Begin by connecting with your body.
Sense your arms and legs.
Sense your belly center.
Take a breath.
Settle into the awareness of your entire body.
Now, call your 2/5 Profile into your awareness.
Connect with it.
Open to the gifts it brings.
Feel the pull of your Conscious Line 2 to be alone.
The urge to be in your own space.
Can you allow yourself to go there?
Can you give yourself time with you?
When you're there, can you allow yourself to sense your unique gifts?
Perhaps stand in awe of them.
Listen and wait.
Feel the desire of your Unconscious Line 5 to serve humanity.
Someone, some situation, needs what you especially have to offer.

Can you imagine waiting for the right time and the right call?

Can you imagine stepping out and offering your magnificent greatness to the world?

Notice as people tell stories about you.

They are projecting on you.

Can you let them?

Can you see they are using you as a mirror?

Their stories have nothing to do with you.

Not the positive ones, where they put you on a pedestal and sing your praises.

Not the negative ones where they trash you in their disappointment.

Can you let the projections pass you by?

Can you remember who you are?

Can you cherish who you are?

Can you stand in the awareness that your gifts are needed treasures?

Humanity awaits you.

You are here to transform the world.

Take a moment and connect with the energy of the 2/5 Profile.

See if it would be ok to ask it for guidance.

What do you need to do to align more deeply with this powerful force?

What wisdom does it have for you?

Thank it.

And then bring your awareness back to your body.

Sense your arms and legs.

Breathe into your belly center.

Be still.

Let your awareness of your 2/5 energy incubate.

Now, take time to anchor your experience by journaling your takeaways.

Note: If you want an audio recording of this meditation, reach out to me with your Profile details at info@clientsandhumandesign.com.

9

THE 3/5 PROFILE

MARTYR/HERETIC

Themes

- The great fixers

- Innovative solutions

- Can sustain trial-and-error process

- Bonds-made-and-broken pattern

- Projected on

- Can become pessimistic

- Need non-repetitive work

- Here to influence strangers of consequence

Entelechy: Through their intrepid trial-and-error exploration, the 3/5 Profile has the challenge and capacity to discover new solutions to humanity's problems. Innovative and influential, they use their charm and seductive powers for the greater good.

Famous 3/5 Profiles

Eckhart Tolle, Mother Theresa, Indira Gandhi, Nancy Pelosi, Lily Tomlin, Angelina Jolie, Julia Roberts, Kate Winslet, Shirley MacLaine, Juliette Binoche, Kirsten Dunst, George Clooney, Alice Cooper, Willie Nelson, Joe DiMaggio, Gayle King, Ella Fitzgerald, Diana Ross, Naomi Osaka, Connie Chung, Thich Nhat Hanh, Anandamayi Ma, Deepak Chopra

Overview

Think of the 3/5 Profile as a resilient, adaptable person who is here to come up with novel solutions. In their trial-and-error process, they often make a mess. Like a kid who takes apart a computer before reassembling, the project may look like a failure to an onlooker. But the 3/5 keeps going until it figures out what works. They bump along in life, continuously finding new ways to improve life and relationships.

People see the 3/5 as saviors and want their help. They project all over the 3/5. If the 3/5 takes the projections (positive or negative) to heart, they're in for trouble. Truly, what people see has very little to do with the 3/5 and everything to do with the person projecting.

The 3/5 can be a bit challenging in relationship as they can pick up and walk away if things aren't to their liking. But they can also stick around if there's authentic room for growth.

With a powerful karma, the 3/5 is here to influence a broad reach of people and leave the world in a better place than they found it.

THE CONSCIOUS LINE 3

The Martyr (The Experimenter)

The Conscious Line 3 is here to determine the next level of possibility on the material plane through experiential experimentation. They are mutating the world. They must try something to see if it works. They then share their discoveries with the world.

The material plane is their playground. They continuously challenge the status quo. They are testing what arises in their path, checking to see if there is a way to improve what's before them. With a love of discovery, they wholeheartedly engage in life. People with a Line 3 Profile are designed to encounter life, question it, and improve it! Criticism is antithetical to their learning style and will hamper their mutative contribution. Instead, the empowering question for the Line 3 is, *What did you learn?*

Relationships are not spared in this learning process. The 3rd Line is looking to see what works and what doesn't work. This activates a bonds-made-and-broken theme. If something is off in a relationship, it's unbearable for the 3rd Line. Their trial-and-error mechanism kicks in. They may need to distance themselves to figure out another approach. It's possible they will come back to find a new way of relating. If there is not a new way, they'll end the relationship to make space for the next experience.

THE UNCONSCIOUS LINE 5

The Heretic (The Illuminator)

Line 5 is considered the highest line of the Hexagram. With a Line 5 in the Profile, the whole chart is taken to a universal level. People with 5th Lines have the enormous job of serving humanity. They have a responsibility. They have influential power. They are the saviors here to solve problems. They are bringing a new light with new solutions. How they go about doing that will depend on which line the Line 5 is paired with. For example, paired with the Line 1, answers become clear through research. Paired with the Line 2, answers are revealed while they're in their *hermitage*. In this case, paired with Line 3, answers are discovered through trial and error. This 3/5 combo brings forth the Crazy Wisdom aspect in what can look like a reckless way.

Regardless of how the Line 5 resolves crises, they are recognized by others as someone who has the capacity to help. They are sought out and called upon. They also call others to them. With a seductive and magnetic pull, they attract the people they are here to serve. Not designed to be solving problems day and night, they are more like the surgeon on call, at the ready, waiting to fulfill their karmic role as saviors.

There are a few challenges here:

The 5th Line is projected on. They are not seen for who they are, rather for who people want them to be. They act as mirrors, showing people what they need to heal in themselves. If the Line 5 is in the wrong place at the wrong time, getting or responding to the wrong projections, they can be the object of negative projections. This can be painful for the Line 5 if they take the projections personally.

If the Line 5 is getting positive projections but then believes the projections to be personally about them, they can get entwined in believing they *are* the savior rather than the bringers of the solution. Also, the Line 5 is designed to bring the solution and then step away. Their job is done. It's time to let others take over. If the Line 5 stays too long the positive projection can turn negative. Likewise, if the Line 5's solution doesn't work, they can be negatively projected on.

Are you beginning to see the challenge? The Line 5 has a natural leadership and broad, influential reach. The name Heretic, points to the 5th Line's challenge of being negatively projected on as they bring new solutions to humanity that may or may not be received or work.

Finally, Line 5 is here to impact strangers of consequence rather than people who they already know. This is the Profile of someone who has karmic relationships. Every meeting with a stranger is potentially life changing. Think of Mother Theresa or Eckhart Tolle.

THE 3/5 PROFILE

When we pair the Conscious, mutative Line 3 with the Unconscious Savior Line 5, we have an extraordinary person, capable of previously unimaginable possibilities. They are the luminary leaders, after all, committed to upgrading life for humanity.

With their Conscious Line 3 they have that brilliant capacity to meet life in full curiosity. Like a child in a sandbox, they're experimenting. They won't hesitate to taste the sand or throw it, for that matter. Always learning, they are continuously engaged in the creative act of discovery. But discovery with a purpose. They are meeting and upgrading life, first and foremost, for themselves. But then the Line 5 kicks in and their exploration takes on meaning. It is for the benefit of humanity. There is a calling that they're responding to. There is a need to fill. They must come up with a new solution. When Einstein said "You can't solve a problem at the level of the problem." He was speaking to this 5th Line energy. New light, new solutions. New ways of seeing what the problem is and how to solve it.

One of my favorite examples of this is my amazing book and business coach Angela Lauria. Always an avid reader, she naturally became a ghostwriter at a young age. Grappling with her own weight issues, she turned to self-help books to explore what might assist her on her journey. At the same time, she was passionate about fighting for the rights of those without a voice. She was committed to righting the wrongs in the world. She was outraged by the effects of institutionalized racism and sexism. She fought for LGBTQ rights. Angela understood the importance of *voice* in this fight. She saw that the publishing industry was based in a male hierarchy. It let only a privileged few have their voice heard. It deemed who was worthy to speak and controlled the dialogue. Angela set out to shift the paradigm by creating The Difference Press and a book writing program, *The Author Incubator*, that welcomed people who were called to make a difference. Angela accepts people who are clear they have a message to share, and she gives them a platform to share it. I was one of the recipients of her visionary, mutative leadership. Angela has a strong Crazy Wisdom aspect. She's breaking down old structures that no longer serve humanity.

With the Conscious Line 3 this 3/5 Profile is included in the group that have a Right Angle Cross. Thus, it has a Personal Destiny. The 3/5's Type, Strategy, and Authority will determine how they best interact with the world given their Profile.

Gifts

The 3/5 Profile is laden with gifts.

Visionary and curious, the 3/5 Profile is here to save the world with new values and new possibilities. They have an unbounded resiliency to explore and learn what works and what doesn't. They have a passion to help others, and a profound wisdom that comes through their lived experience.

My Tibetan Buddhist dharma teacher, Lama Palden, has a 3/5 Profile. She was one of the first Western women to enter the rigorous traditional Tibetan Buddhist three-year retreat with Kalu Rinpoche. Following the retreat, she established Sukhasiddhi, an organization dedicated to easing the suffering of humanity through the Shangpa Kagyu Tibetan Buddhist practices. With permission, Lama Palden experimented with teaching elements of the three-year-retreat to Western laypeople, spread out over a longer period time. She began the first training that enabled laypeople to get these extraordinary teachings while still working and raising children. I had the great fortune being one of twelve students in the second group of what was initially called The Six Year Program (which extended well beyond that!). We committed to meditating and doing the practices two hours a day along with a series of longer retreats. Through this program, Lama Palden brought a new solution, a new way to access these profound teachings in a format that was doable for people unable to take three years off to retreat.

My essential oil mentor, Greg Toews, also has a 3/5 Profile. He tells moving stories of his trials and tribulations as a young person trying to figure out life. Some of his experiments left him with ongoing body challenges including a broken back that should have left him in a wheelchair. As he met teachers and was initiated into various spiritual domains, he began a thirty-year exploration of essential oils and healing modalities. Currently, he is a remarkable *pranic* healer, the CEO of Astara, and a cutting-edge leader in the world of essential oils. Greg is influencing people throughout the world through his teachings and organization, Plant Prana. Again, I feel very fortunate to be the recipient of his lifelong exploration as he brings new solutions in the healing realms.

Challenges

The challenges for the 3/5 can be onerous.

First, there is the challenge of the Line 3: not knowing if something is going to work until you try it. Pair that with the Line 5's burden of people always expecting you to come through with a solution, and if you don't get it right, you get walloped. That combination makes the projection field especially dicey for the 3/5 Profile.

If the 3/5 is thinking they should be perfect and get things right immediately, they will suffer. In the same way, it can be agonizing if other people are judging them, and the 3/5 takes it personally. The 3/5 Profile can doubt themselves and buy into the story that they are a failure. There's just a lot of experimentation that can easily be viewed as mistakes and disappointments by the broad group people looking to the 3/5 in a leadership capacity.

That brings us to the challenge of being wise when deciding which problem-solving calls to accept. If the 3/5 is not following their Strategy and leaps to help in a situation that is not right for them, they will have that experience of falling from grace – a kind of splat. Talk to any 3/5 and they will recognize this experience in their lives.

Then, there is that issue of relationships.

The 3/5 has the bonds-made-and-broken theme with a trial-and-error process. This theme permeates relationships as well as in other parts of their lives. If something doesn't feel good in relationship, it's unbearable. The 3/5 is designed to move away from what doesn't work and move towards what does. They can leave relationships abruptly if they don't see a way to influence an untenable situation. This can be challenging for the person they're in relationship with, who can feel unreasonably dumped. It can also be difficult for the 3/5 Profile, who lives in a world that says pair bonding is the ultimate happiness.

There is good news for those 3/5 Profiles who desire long-term relationships. If the partner can tolerate the 3/5 coming and going while they find what they need and what works, the relationship can become stable and viable.

It can be tough having a 3/5 Profile, especially before you realize the power of the gift you've been given. Take my sister's child Emily, who had a 3/5 Profile. Always projected on, my then niece felt tremendous pressure to get things right. An incredible artist, nothing was ever good enough (always in process of upgrading). Relationships as a 3/5 were confounded by the fact that her Human Design Type was a Manifestor. Brilliant as she was, Emily couldn't seem to get to a comfortable place in relationships. With puberty came a sense of helplessness and, ultimately, a realization that she was in fact a *he*. Shifting identities from Emily to Finn, he began the exploration of transforming his body into a more aligned experience of himself. But the body experiment was cut short when the new experiment became one of exploring death. Again, people with 3/5 Profiles must embody the experiment to discover if it's a mistake or not. I do not believe Finn actually wanted to die. I believe it was an experiment gone awry.

(Note: I use Finn's deadname with his permission.)

WORKING WITH A 3/5 PROFILE

You have a client who has a 3/5 Profile!

Hang on to your hat! You're most likely in for a ride...

First things first: Don't judge anything your 3/5 client does. Always gear them towards the question, *What did you learn from this experiment?*

The 3/5 learns by trial and error. They need the space to explore and discover. They need the room to have things not work so they can discover what does work. It could be easy to see the mess they may present as a problem. Don't fall prey to projections!

Consider the challenge the younger 3/5 Profile may have in managing the tension between the Line 3 and the Line 5. They feel the pressure to save the world and yet seem to fail at every turn. Or they are continuously put on a pedestal that they know is not authentic and feel the pressure to live up to a projection.

My most successful 3/5 clients have learned to fully embrace their trial-and-error style. In fact, they relish it. They understand that there are no mistakes. They value the wisdom gained from trying things out. They don't think in terms of failure.

If your coach has a 3/5 Profile (like my writing and business coach Angela Lauria), they will teach trial and error as *The Way*. Be clear, you can learn from that style even if it is not your own natural Profile path. Working with Angela has brought more room for experimentation into my life. It has tempered some of my paralyzing perfectionism. The theme with Angela is always *Try it! See if works. If it doesn't, try something else!* That said, if you do not have a 3rd Line in your Profile, then trial and error is not your long suit. By all means, use it, but tune into your unique strengths.

If the issue your client faces is a relationship issue, remember that with the 5th Line, the 3/5 Profile rarely lets people see who they truly are. Because of the propensity for people to project on them, they tend to hide out. In partnerships, hold the possibility of the 3/5 working it out, but don't expect the 3/5 to stick around. With a bonds-made-and-broken theme, they are always looking to have the relationship feel right. When it doesn't, they move on. Know that if the 3/5's partner can be spacious with the 3/5's process, the chance of a longer-term relationship increases exponentially.

I was speaking with a coach today about her Projector virtual assistant. She was wondering how to work with her more effectively. I asked what her Profile was. Turns out she is a 3/5. We talked about giving her a mission she can get behind and a problem she can solve. Call her out. Give her full permission to engage her trial-and-error process. Let her find out what does work by discovering what doesn't. This information gave my client more space and a sense of ease in working with her assistant.

GUIDED MEDITATION

Imagine for a moment that you are a unique, once-in-a-lifetime being brought to Earth with a special mission. You have an important purpose. You are bringing an invaluable piece to the larger puzzle of humanity. Your light cannot be replicated by anyone else.

To ignite your purpose and ensure that your light is turned on, you've been given a gift: your Profile. You have been gifted the 3/5 Profile. This Profile provides insight into how to realize your potential. It shows you the mechanism or the learning style that will call forth your purpose.

Take a moment.
Put everything aside.
Let the past fall away.
Let the future dissolve.
Turn your attention to the present moment.
Allow your awareness to shift from ordinary consciousness
    to extraordinary consciousness.
Begin by connecting with your body.
Sense your arms and legs.
Sense your belly center.
Take a breath.
Settle into the awareness of your entire body.
Now call your 3/5 Profile into your awareness.
Feel the curiosity of your Conscious Line 3.

So alive!

So willing to experiment.

Feel how compelled it is to discover what works and what doesn't.

Sense the creative freedom to explore!

Now, turn to the Unconscious Line 5.

What do you notice? Can you feel the enormous job the Line 5 has?

Do you recognize that you are here to solve problems?

That you have the task of saving the world?

How does that feel?

Is it a relief to acknowledge it?

Does it feel like a burden you carry?

Now look around at the people who want your help.

Who needs what you have to offer?

Can you see that you are calling them to you?

Can you feel them projecting onto you?

Are they positive projections?

Or have you disappointed someone and are being hit with negative projections?

Can you see them for what they are: projections?

How would it be to not take the projections personally?

Take a moment and appreciate your 3/5 Profile.

What do you love about it?

What do you find challenging?

Would it be OK to turn to it as a wisdom energy and ask it if it has any guidance for you?

If so, what does it say?

Take a moment and receive the 3/5's gifts.

Take a moment to forgive yourself for any explorations that seemingly ran amuck.

Recognize that every apparent mistake you've made has led you closer to your goal.

Feel the power of your 3/5 Profile.

Take a moment to honor it.
Recognize it as your path.
Ask to be in alignment with it.
Thank it.
Now, bring your awareness back into your body.
Sense your arms and legs.
Breathe into your belly center.
Be still.
Let your awareness of your 3/5 energy incubate.
Now, take time to anchor your experience by journaling your takeaways.

Note: If you want an audio recording of this meditation, reach out to me with your Profile details at info@clientsandhumandesign.com.

10

THE 3/6 PROFILE

MARTYR/ROLE MODEL

Themes

- Triphasic

- Engage in trial-and-error process to embody wisdom

- Trust, perfection, and indecision are big issues

- Bonds-made-and-broken pattern

- Looking for their soulmate

- Here to impact strangers of consequence

Entelechy: The highly mutative 3/6 Profile brings powerful transformation through experience. With tenacious resilience, they compost negative experiences into wisdom. As the Role Models of living true to one's inner authority, they inspire humanity to embrace authenticity.

Famous 3/6 Profiles

Robert Bly, Mariah Carey, Margaux Hemingway, Kate Hudson, Elizabeth Clare Prophet, Charlene Spretnak, Lawrence Welk, Dustin Hoffman, Joan Cusack, Tina Fey, Thomas Merton, Carrie Underwood

Overview

The Conscious Line 3 and the Unconscious Line 6 are in a harmonic. Both are looking for truth, though they approach it from different angles. The Conscious Line 3 discovers truth by experimentation. Through an experiential, hands-on, messy encounter with life, they determine what works by hitting up against what doesn't work. This is their natural trial-and-error process. This is how they gain wisdom. The Unconscious Line 6 is born into the world with an innate knowing. They have the long view of life. They are witnesses. They are looking for integrity, for alignment, and for perfection in life. Their approach is detached. They are looking to determine what's possible when they live in alignment with their authenticity.

Together, these two lines take the triphasic journey through life.

• For the first thirty years, they explore life as a double Line 3. Remember the Line 6 acts like a Line 3 for those first thirty years. This is a period of learning by experimentation. It can be a steep learning curve for the 3/6 Profile as they bump into life and discover what doesn't work. This is also a time of encountering relationships and breaking off relationships in their discovery process.

• From age thirty to fifty, the Unconscious Line 6 goes on the roof and takes a witnessing stance. This can be supportive and a slight reprieve for the Line 3, which continues to learn by trial and error but also gets some perspective and support from the Line 6 vantage.

• Sometime around age fifty (at their Kiron Return), there is an integration process. The Role Model phase kicks in and the trial-and-error learnings are integrated along with the witnessing insights. There is a maturity and wisdom as the 3/6 embodies their hard-won sagacity. Even then, the Conscious Line 3 remains active and engages the 3/6 in a personal exploration and discovery process.

The tension between the two lines can bring a tendency towards indecision. The Line 6 may hold the Line 3 back from exploration. While the Line 3 has a personal life theme, the Line 6 has a transpersonal pull and is here to impact strangers of consequence. Likewise, while the Line 3 has a self-absorbed nature, the Line 6 is looking for their soulmate.

THE CONSCIOUS LINE 3

The Martyr (The Experimenter)

The Conscious Line 3 is here to determine the next level of possibility on the material plane by exploring life. They must try something to see if it works. They then share their discoveries with the world.

Perpetual learners, the Line 3 is fully engaged in life. Their insatiable curiosity drives them to explore and improve anything in their path. They are here to experience life's display and change it as they see fit. Someone with a 3rd Line should never be criticized nor criticize themselves. Instead, the empowering question for the Line 3 is, *What did you learn?*

In relationship, there can be a bonds-made-and-broken theme. If something is not working in a relationship, they feel it and need to transform it. They may pull away temporarily to reconnect with themselves and evaluate what is not working. Often, they return offering a new way of relating. If they cannot find a way to be authentic, the relationship will fall away. This creates an opening for the next level of coherence they seek.

THE UNCONSCIOUS LINE 6

The Role Model

The Unconscious Line 6 brings the eagle's view. It has a witnessing capacity that sees into the future and understands things that others haven't quite caught up to. It can be distressing for the Line 6 when what is obvious to them is not yet apparent to others. Understanding this challenge can alleviate the propensity to judge those who do not have the long view as well as the propensity to question themselves when they are not understood. Because this is the Unconscious aspect, they may not fully realize what is bothering them.

There is also a natural quality of detachment with the Line 6. They are standing back and watching life, especially after age thirty. This keeps them on the edge of a group rather than stepping into the inner circle.

THE 3/6 PROFILE

What an interesting dynamic when these two lines meet! It's like they have two different personalities, even though they want the same thing. They're both going for truth but from different perspectives. The Line 3 wants and needs to jump into the fray while the Line 6 wants to stand back and observe.

During the first thirty years of their life, the Unconscious Line 6 functions like a Line 3. So, they essentially live in a double Line 3 configuration. That is a ton of trial-and-error energy. As a result, the 3/6 Profile can feel without direction during this period.

Look at Robert Bly's life, for example. True to the double Line 3 form, he spent until he was about thirty going from one experience to the next. He first spent two years in the Navy followed by a year at Olaf College in Minnesota, at which point he transferred to Harvard, where he was part of group of famous writers. From there, he went to the University of Iowa Writers Workshop for another two years.

If we follow Bly through the triphasic process, we see that at thirty, he got a Fullbright grant to go to Norway and translate Norwegian poetry into English. It was in this second phase that he got a larger view and some ground in his life. He discovered poets that were not known in the United States, including Pablo Neruda. In response, Bly started a literary magazine to translate these poets and introduce them to the United States.

As he entered his Role Model phase, he embodied his knowledge, writing copious poems and penning his international bestselling work *Iron John: A Book About Men*. As a leader, he became known for his experiential workshops for men.

If we think about poetry for a moment, it embodies the tension in these two lines. It is at once offering an expanded view and a wisdom view. Poetry plummets the reader into a lived experience to discover and witness some truth.

This tension between Line 3 and Line 6 plays out in relationships as well. The Conscious 3rd Line has a bonds-made-and-broken theme. They are engaging with people then separating. Meanwhile, the Unconscious 6th Line is looking for their soulmate. The 3rd Line needs exploration; the 6th Line craves a more stable relationship.

Mariah Carrey is known as "the Songbird Supreme." With a five-octave vocal range, her celebrated musical talent has touched the world. If you look at Mariah Carrey's life, you will see the Conscious Line 3 totally engaged in both her music career and her many relationships. Musically, she tried new styles of songs over the years with different songwriting partners. She also changed record labels numerous times as she grew unhappy with them. Relationally, she has been married or with new partners every two to six years. This is not a judgment; it's a reflection of the 6th Line wanting to be in relationship, looking for their soulmate. Meanwhile, the 3rd Line is doing its job of finding out what doesn't work in a partnership so they can discover what does. To say it another way, the 3rd Line is somewhat pessimistic and looking for what's wrong to figure out what's right, while the 6th Line has a positive outlook and is in search of perfection.

The 3/6 Profile is also part of the group that have a Right Angle Cross. Thus, it has a Personal Destiny. Their Type, Strategy, and Authority will determine how they best interact with the world given their Profile.

Gifts

The 3/6 brings an invaluable gift. They are embodying wisdom through their experience of life. They call us to live authentically from a place of truth. They also have a tenacious resilience coupled with a capacity to stay the course as they bump around. At their best, they have the ability to learn from and harvest negative experiences, then bring that wisdom as a leader. They teach an alternative model of maturation that embraces "mistakes" as necessary compost for future harvests.

Take my colleague, friend, and bestselling author Vera LaRee.

Vera was born into a polygamist cult in Mexico in 1971. One of fifty-seven siblings (her father had eleven wives), Vera was taught that women were inferior to men and God was to be feared. From an early age, she was manipulated, brainwashed, and sexually violated. Married at sixteen, she began having children of her own. In 2002 (during that second phase), she escaped to the United States with her three children, a suitcase of clothes, and $500 to her name. Here, she built a multimillion-dollar business. Vera had a long-view vision and the perseverance to live her truth. Her Line 6 would not let her stay trapped. Her Line 3 enabled her to explore ways to escape. She says her mission is to help women and men identify whatever is keeping them trapped in their lives so they can finally break free from what she calls their personal cult.

Challenges

There are challenges that come with this 3/6 energy.

For one, trust is very important. The Line 6 has high standards in relationship. They are looking for perfection and integrity in life. It's very important for them to be able to trust people. The Line 6 values safety. They like to stand back. They get ground from the witnessing position.

Meanwhile, the Line 3 has a different agenda. It needs to explore. It needs to experience life. It's messy. It needs to touch the hot stove to know not to touch it. Witnessing won't do. Line 3 defies safety. If Line 6 is holding Line 3 back, it can lead to a stalled situation or indecision. Indecision is a common theme that is part of the 3/6 Profile territory. Another difference the two lines must face are their views on life. The Line 6 holds a positive view of life. Line 3 leans towards pessimism. These differences have to be navigated. Ultimately, the pessimism of the 3rd Line can be overcome when their trial-and-error process is embraced as crucial to their development of wisdom.

More challenges can arise with these two lines in the area of relationship. We spoke about this above, but it's worth repeating. The Line 3 has a bonds-made-and-broken theme, while Line 6 is looking for their soulmate. If a relationship is not right for the Line 3, it's not right. End of story. Not that the Line 3 couldn't come back to the relationship to see if something has changed, but the Line 3 needs its discovery space.

Of course, there is always the challenge for the 3/6 to follow their Strategy and Authority. If the 3rd Line takes off on a trial-and-error trip that is not right for it, they can mess up. As long as they are harvesting what they learn, they can use the mess up to get back on track. However, if they get trapped in believing they have made an error, they can get stuck in a negative, self-deprecating eddy.

WORKING WITH A 3/6 PROFILE

When you are working with a person with the 3/6 Profile think in terms of a maturing process. The 3/6 is on the trajectory to embody wisdom through the combination of trial-and-error learning, witnessing, and recognizing their innate wisdom.

To begin, consider where they are in the triphasic life cycle. Give them this perspective on their life. Acknowledge the tension between the Line 3 and the Line 6. What is their experience of these two lines in their life?

Encourage the reframe of the Line 3 exploration process as a necessary asset. Point out that exploration is a support to the Line 6 even if it feels threatening. Help them to harvest their "errors" rather than be defeated by them. Byron Katie has a saying: *Look forward to it (the thing you don't want to have happen/don't want to experience)!* You thrive when you're clear that you're here to learn from what doesn't work rather than judge yourself for making what appears to be a mistake.

That said, work with their Strategy and Authority to help

them be clear in terms of what to explore and when. Affirm that their task is to accumulate experiences that are in alignment with them. Explain that the Line 3 is self-absorbed while the Line 6 is aware of others. Encourage them to allow their Line 3 self-absorption as a necessary aspect of their wisdom gathering. Most of all, help them to understand that their drive for truth and authenticity must be navigated from various angles.

GUIDED MEDITATION

Imagine for a moment that you are a unique, once-in-a-lifetime being brought to Earth with a particular mission. You have an important purpose. You are here to bring an invaluable piece to the larger puzzle of humanity. Your light cannot be replicated by anyone else.

To ignite your purpose and ensure that your light is turned on, you've been given a gift: your Profile. You have been gifted the 3/6 Profile. This Profile gives you insight into how to realize your potential. It shows you the mechanism or the learning style that will call forth your purpose.

> *Take a moment to let go of the past and shift your focus to the present moment.*
> *Allow your awareness to shift from ordinary consciousness to extraordinary consciousness.*
> *You are turning on the light of awareness to explore your 3/6 Profile.*
> *Begin by sensing your arms and legs.*
> *Let yourself arrive in your body.*
> *Breathe into your belly center.*
> *Gently stretch to find a comfortable resting place.*
> *Now, open to the Conscious Line 3 of your Profile.*
> *Recognize yourself as someone who is here to learn by thoroughly engaging in life.*

*You need to try things out to see what doesn't work so you
     can get clear on what does.*

You are gathering much-needed information.

There are no mistakes here.

*Only information you learn that brings you closer to
     truth.*

Now, bring your awareness to your Unconscious 6th Line.

Which phase of life are you in?

*Are you in your first thirty years of life where the 6th Line
     acts like the 3rd Line?*

If so, you are finding your way by trial and error.

Can you allow yourself to bump around?

*Can you turn to your Strategy and Authority for
     guidance?*

*Or are you in the second phase of your 6th Line Profile –
     roughly age thirty to fifty?*

*Here, your Line 6 has gone on the roof, and you are
     learning through witnessing.*

*Notice how your Line 3 gets some ground with this new
     perspective.*

*Perhaps you're in the last phase of life – from fifty
     onwards?*

*Here, you have integrated what you've learned through
     trial and error and from witnessing.*

Are you embodying your Role Model self?

How does it feel?

*Take a moment to recognize Line 3 and Line 6 in action
     together.*

*Feel how the Conscious Line 3 has the up close and
     personal information.*

Notice how the Unconscious Line 6 has a long vision.

Feel the Conscious Line 3's tendency to want to jump in.

Feel the Unconscious Line 6's tendency to hang back.

How are you navigating that difference?

Smile at your 3/6 Profile.
Ask it if there is any information your 3/6 Profile has
for you.
Thank it.
And when you're ready, gently bring your awareness back
to your body.
Sense your arms and legs.
Sense your belly center.
Take a breath.
Slowly bring your awareness back into the room.
Be still. Let what you have received integrate.
Take some time to anchor your experience by writing about
it in your journal.

Note: If you want an audio recording of this meditation, reach out to me with your Profile details at info@clientsandhumandesign.com.

11

THE 4/6 PROFILE

OPPORTUNIST/ROLE MODEL

Themes

• The only profile with both lines in the upper, transpersonal trigram

• Line 4 is in tension with the Line 6 – Line 4 is social and engaged while Line 6 stands back with the larger view

• Has the 6th Line triphasic experience of life

• Can get exhausted by being around people and must step back at times

• Friendships are important – 4/6 Profiles have the capacity to develop genuine authentic intimate relationships

• Not necessarily here to be impacted by people but are waiting to impact people

Entelechy: The remarkable 4/6 Profile has the possibility to be a role model and leader that impacts a large network of people by living true to themselves. Friendly and generous, their wisdom opens vistas and alters people's thinking.

Famous 4/6 Profiles

Dalai Lama, Dolly Parton, Prince Charles, Joe Biden, Pete Buttigieg, Robert Kennedy, Eleanor Roosevelt, Picasso, Brad Pitt, Whitney Houston, Gloria Estefan, Ravi Shankar

Overview

The 4/6 has the interesting mix of being the only profile with both lines in the upper transpersonal trigram yet at the same time, they have a personal destiny. In other words, they interact with life in relation to their own personal process.

Everything about the 4/6 is a bit unusual.

The Line 4 and the Line 6 are somewhat at odds with each other. Line 4 is interested in connection; Line 6 likes to stand back and witness. Line 4 is nourished by friendships; Line 6 can get exhausted by all the contact.

During the Line 6's triphasic experience of life, it goes through different relationships with the Line 4:

• There is a tension during the first thirty years, when the Line 6 is in the Line 3 phase. During that time, Line 4 is needing stability, while Line 3 is exploring and discovering life and learning through experimentation.

• During the second phase, from roughly thirty to fifty, things shift. Here, the Line 4 gets ground and support from the witnessing vantage of the Line 6 on the roof. The sense of security is also being nourished in this phase of life as Line 4 is actively establishing a network through work, family, and friends.

• During third phase, around age fifty until death, Line 4 re-enters the network with their wisdom self. They integrate their *Role Model/Adept* in the community. This a potent and powerful mix.

The combination of relational intimacy and leadership is compelling with a disarming potential. People with this configuration can speak in a leadership role to large numbers of people in a very personal way. Picture Dolly Parton, Eleanor Roosevelt, and the Dalai Lama, and you can get a sense of the 4/6's potential power through intimacy.

THE CONSCIOUS LINE 4

The Opportunist (The Connector)

The Conscious Line 4 is the first of the interpersonal lines. It is gathering information about relationships with the ultimate intent to make a worthy contribution. As the foundational line for the upper trigram, it has a quality of insecurity coupled with the drive to establish security.

Deeply relational, the Conscious Line 4 Profile has a need for an established community and a strong network. You could say that their lives depend on their network. It is through their network that they meet the people that are aligned partners. It is through their network that they're offered jobs. It is through their network that they hear about the best homes. We could say their network is their pot of gold. They also have a unique capacity to impact people on a personal level through their network.

THE UNCONSCIOUS LINE 6

The Role Model

The Unconscious Line 6 has the long view of life. An old soul, it has a witnessing capacity that sees into the future and understands things that others haven't yet recognized. This can be confusing for the person with a Line 6 in their Profile. Understanding their capacity can alleviate judgement of others as well as the impulse to question themselves when they are not understood.

There is also a natural quality of detachment with the Line 6. They are standing back and watching life, especially after thirty. Typically, they stand at the edge of a group as a witness rather than stepping into the inner circle as a participant.

Triphasic

Line 6 has that triphasic quality, giving them the opportunity to experience life from different vantages as they gain their wisdom.

• For their first thirty years, the person with a Line 6 Profile lives the life of a Line 3. Life is one big experiment. They are discovering, through trial and error, what does and doesn't work. This is an embodied kind of learning. They must touch the stove to learn that it is, in fact, hot and burns! Warning them is not enough. It's a bit of a wild ride that can look and feel like one mistake after another. Each of those "mistakes" is an opportunity for rich learning, creating a knowledge base for later years.

• Having spent the first thirty years deep in hands-on experimentation, the Line 6 then shifts gears. From about age thirty to fifty, they step back from the fire of learning by trial and error and become the observer. From this vantage, they gain perspective on life. Here, they are witnessing what works and what doesn't work. They are continuing to build their data base of wisdom and clarity, this time from afar.

• When the 6th Line reaches their Kiron Return around age fifty and for the remainder of their lives, they embody the *Role Model*. However, to harvest their full capacity to share their Role Model wisdom with the world, they must embrace and integrate what they've learned in the first two phases.

THE 4/6 PROFILE

When we combine the Conscious Line 4 with the Unconscious Line 6 there is an alchemical process that is hard to articulate. The Line 4 and the Line 6 are like a marriage that's not quite a fit, and yet works in some amazing and empowering way. The differences between these two lines and the journey they take over time create a very special person.

People with a 4/6 Profile are at once contained within themselves at the same time they have a quality of intimacy that calls for contact. Their leadership capabilities are always evident even though their leadership sometimes appears as a background fragrance or backdrop. I always get the feeling I'm with someone solid when I'm around a 4/6 – someone I can count on. It's almost as if the 4/6 has an adult in the house – at least, once they're past thirty.

Those first thirty years can be a bit of a ride while their Line 6 acts like a Line 3, bumping into life and making messes. This is in direct opposition to the 4th Line during that time that is desperately trying to keep things stable. Fortunately, these energies can find their way to work together and support one another in the final two phases of life. Unfortunately, this isn't always the outcome. Whitney Houston never got the chance to live her life as the Role Model she was born to be. She died just before turning fifty.

The 4/6 has a mission. They are bringing wisdom to their network. It's serious business but done through friendliness. The Dalai Lama is such a great example. He's so likable, so friendly, so unassuming, and so playful. And yet he travels the world with the very serious mission to alleviate suffering and bring joy to humanity.

Typically, we think of people with Line 4 as averse to change. What I've noticed with the 4/6 is that the long view of the Line 6 can act as a stabilizing force, enabling the Line 4 to tolerate change that might be unbearable for the other Line 4 Profiles.

The 4/6 Profile is the last of the Profiles that have a Right Angle Cross. Even though both its Conscious and Unconscious lines are in the upper trigram, it has a Personal Destiny. I don't exactly understand the logic there, but that is the case. So, like the other Right Angle crosses, people with a 4/6 Profile are here to be absorbed in themselves and to explore their personal experience of life rather than exploring other people's processes. Their Type, Strategy, and Authority will determine how they best interact with the world given their Profile.

Gifts

Never underestimate someone with a 4/6 Profile. They are wise visionaries with big hearts. Ahead of their time, they have the enviable gift of bringing their foresight down to earth in a intimate and relational way. Their gift of friendliness and their capacity to connect with people make them trustworthy and reliable. When they are aligned, they have the potential to bring their message to a large and expansive network.

Five years ago, my wife and I were vacationing at Indian Rocks Beach on the Gulf Coast of Florida, where we met a mature couple from Indiana. It was around the time of the presidential elections, and our conversation turned to politics. The couple told us at that time to keep an eye out for their mayor, Pete Buttigieg. We had never heard of him. They could not say enough about him. He was going places, they said. Sure enough, Pete stepped into the limelight when he made a presidential run four years later. Pete's personal impact and networking aura were fast at work long before he came into the world's view. His wisdom and heart inspired this couple, and they were passing the flame.

Challenges

The challenges of the 4/6 Profile begin with their first thirty years when their Line 6 and Line 4 are in conflict. During this time frame, Line 6 acts like a Line 3, learning by trial and error. At the same time, Line 4 is trying to stabilize their lives and relationships. This is an "oil and water" scenario and can create challenging internal conflicts for the 4/6.

The next challenge is the difference between the two lines. Line 4 wants to connect. Line 6 wants to keep its distance. Who wins? How does that play out? It's a relationship that has to be navigated within the person.

Another challenge is the Line 6, having that long view, knows things ahead of other people. They want to bring their wisdom to their network, but often, they have to wait a good twenty years before what they know can be heard.

My friend and colleague, Human Design consultant, practitioner, and author Charlotte Friborg, had this 4/6 experience. Twenty years ago, in Denmark, she rode her bike to a green bin to recycle her garbage. People laughed at her, saying, "What difference does one person make?" Now, everyone in Denmark recycles in a very organized and efficient way. She could see then what needed to be done to make a difference. It frustrates her to no end that her condo complex in Florida has two green bins for an entire complex. She's like, *Come on people. Let's get going!* Charlotte is clear she must have her network in place before she can bring her message, and only then when the timing is right.

Finally, if the 4/6 does not have a good network, things can get gnarly. They need the container within which to share their message. If they do not have a good network, everything in their lives can be off kilter. They don't meet the right people to form relationships. They don't get the right jobs. They don't get the right homes. When we say the Line 4 is as good as their network, well, we mean it.

WORKING WITH A 4/6 PROFILE

When you are working with the 4/6 Profile begin by recognizing you have a leader in your midst – a visionary. Don't doubt or question their view of things. Be curious to learn what they know. Support them to embrace the power and possibility they hold. Take note of where they are in the triphasic life cycle. Help the 4/6 understand and reflect on those phases.

Kelly Hanson has a 4/6 Profile. She is an author, colleague, and a Human Design student who said,

"My 6th Line is interesting. I definitely would not have pinned myself as someone who needs to learn through experiences, but that is how my life played out in my earlier years. Although I would not trade the hard-earned lessons that I learned or where I ended up, I certainly would not pick to redo some of my life experiences, especially my teenage years."

Have your 4/6 client reflect on their life phases. Where are they? What have they learned? Have them consider their network. Is it supporting them? Do they need to find a new network? What kind of network would support them?

Kelly spoke about her experience finding her network this way:

"I now see how important the people I am with and the places I am in can be. Who I was at the core of my being never changed, but how I expressed it and my relationship with myself was affected by my surroundings. It is almost like the 4th Line could be compared to a houseplant not receiving the right amount of light and water to thrive. The plant may not be aware that its environment is causing it not to thrive, it will keep growing, even in its stunted way. Once it is moved into a better place, it will not just put its energy into surviving; rather, it will begin to thrive."

GUIDED MEDITATION

Imagine for a moment that you are a unique, once-in-a-lifetime being brought to Earth with a particular mission. You have an important purpose. What you have to bring is invaluable to the larger puzzle of humanity. Your light cannot be replicated by anyone else.

To ignite your purpose and ensure that your light is turned on, you've been given a gift, your Profile. You have been gifted the 4/6 Profile. This Profile gives you insight into how to realize your potential. It shows you the mechanism or the learning style that will call forth your purpose.

> Take a moment to let go of the past and bring your focus to
>   the present moment.
> Allow your awareness to shift from ordinary consciousness
>   to extraordinary consciousness.
> You are turning on the light of awareness to explore your
>   4/6 Profile.
> Begin by sensing your arms and legs.
> Let yourself arrive in your body.

Take a breath into your belly center.

Gently stretch to find a comfortable resting place.

Now, open to the Conscious Line 4 of your Profile.

Recognize yourself as someone who is friendly, relational, and connected to people.

Notice how important your network is to you.

Do your partnerships, your business, your homes all come through your network?

If not, would you consider expanding your network?

Shift your awareness to your Unconscious 6th line.

Which phase of life are you in?

Are you in your first thirty years of life where your Line 6 acts like the Line 3?

If so, you are finding your way by trial and error.

How is your Line 4's need for stability faring during this time?

Or are you in the second phase of your Line 6 Profile – roughly age thirty to fifty?

Here, your Line 6 has gone on the roof, and you are learning through witnessing.

Notice how much more harmonious this is for your Line 4!

Perhaps you're in the last phase of life – from fifty onwards?

Here you have integrated what you learned through trial and error and from witnessing?

Are you bringing your wisdom to the tribe and to your community?

How does that feel?

Take a moment to recognize your Conscious Line 4 and your Unconscious Line 6 together.

Feel your Conscious Line 4's enthusiasm to interact with people.

Feel your Unconscious Line 6's long vision.

Feel the desire to bring what you know to your community.

And feel your Line 6's tendency to hang back.
How are you navigating that difference?
Smile at your 4/6 Profile.
Ask it if there is any information your Profile has for you.
Thank it.
And when you're ready, gently bring your awareness back
to your body.
Sense your arms and legs.
Sense your belly center.
Take a breath.
And slowly bring your awareness back into the room.
Be still. Let what you have received integrate.
Take some time to anchor your experience by writing about
it in your journal.

Note: If you want an audio recording of this meditation, reach out to me with your Profile details at info@clientsandhumandesign.com.

THE 4/1 PROFILE

OPPORTUNIST/INVESTIGATOR

Themes

• Two percent of the population

• Connected and extroverted versus introspective and introverted

• Security and insecurity

• Fixed fate

• Study and knowledge with intent to share

• Network is everything

• Here to impact people on a personal level

Entelechy: The rare 4/1 jewel has the gift of being themselves regardless of the situation they're in. They bring the stability of the oak tree to humanity coupled with a deep desire to share their discoveries of life.

Famous 4/1 Profiles

Barbara Walters, Andrew Lloyd Weber, Bette Midler, Claude Monet, Larry Bird, Jean Shinoda Bolen, Tom Brady, Ellen Burstyn, Catharina Amalia Princess of Orange (Netherlands), Gurumayi Chidvilasananda, Angela Davis, Zsa Zsa Gabor, Lyndon B. Johnson, Art Linkletter, Peter Sellers, Shel Silverstein, Louis Vuitton, Stevie Wonder

Overview

The 4/1 Profile is highly unusual. Less than 2 percent of the population fall into this category.

Remember, we divide the Profiles into three groups. The Right Angle Crosses have a personal fate: Profiles 1/3, 1/4, 2/4, 2/5, 3/5, 3/6, and 4/6. The Left Angle Crosses have a transpersonal fate: Profiles 5/1, 5/2, 6/2, and 6/3. Then, there is the solo Juxtaposition Cross, which is the 4/1 Profile.

This Cross is neither personal nor transpersonal. It has its own way of navigating the world.

Think of the 4/1 on a train track going in a singular direction. Their direction and their purpose are determined by their Incarnation Cross, namely the Conscious and Unconscious Sun and Earth. If you're a 4/1 or working with a 4/1, that information will be tremendously valuable.

The important thing to hold in mind with the 4/1 is that they are who they are. If you want to be in relationship with them, you must meet them where they are. They are not designed to abandon themselves to please you.

People with a 4/1 Profile are incredibly friendly and social, yet they need their solitude. They need that alone time to do the big work of being absorbed in learning what intrigues them. They are here to influence people in their network in a very personal way and to get what they need to survive and thrive in life through the people in their network.

THE CONSCIOUS LINE 4

The Opportunist (The Connector)

The Conscious Line 4 is the first of the interpersonal lines. Remember, Line 4 and Line 1 are in a harmonic. While the Unconscious Line 1 is investigating and gathering information about the material world, the Conscious Line 4 is gathering information about relationships. They're working in the same investigative way, only in different areas. Like the Line 1, Line 4 has a quality of insecurity. Change can be unsettling. They do best when they know the next steps. Whether it is a change in relationship, work, or home, it's better for them to know where they're headed.

Deeply relational, the Line 4 has a friendliness about them that draws people to them. The ultimate networkers, they flourish when they are in the correct network. Everything they need for nourishment and sustainability (their jobs, their relationships, and their homes) all come through their network. People with a 4th Line have a unique capacity to impact people on a personal level. I think of them as the whisperers. They are here to touch people's lives one person at a time.

THE UNCONSCIOUS LINE 1

The Investigator

Like Line 4, Line 1 is a bit insecure. Line 1 looks to information to provide ground. With the necessary knowledge, they can make sense of life. Information puts Line 1 at ease. Line 1 needs time on their own absorbed in research. Becoming well educated on a topic that speaks to them is deeply gratifying. Ultimately, they can become a stabilizing force for others as they offer the vast wealth of resources they've gained through study.

THE 4/1 PROFILE

When we pair the Conscious Line 4 with the Unconscious Line 1, we have two lines that are working in a harmonic. Both lines are investigating life, looking for information. The Line 4 at a transpersonal level and the Line 1 at a personal level. Both the Line 4 and the Line 1 have the theme of insecurity. They're looking for a foundation and need information or knowledge to establish that foundation. Line 4 will gather that information by being in relationship. Highly social, they need connection with others in order to fulfill their purpose. Line 1 gathers information while they're in their own world, absorbed in something that fascinates them.

Until the 4/1 has done their investigative work and come to rest in their own inner authority they can feel a bit unsure of themselves. However, even with that insecurity, they have a secure or grounded nature. Like an oak tree, they stand strong in themselves. It's an interesting dynamic. They may feel internally unsure yet they bring stability.

Again, the Conscious Line 4 is deeply relational while the Unconscious Line 1 is concerned with themselves. That leaves a person navigating an extroverted aspect of themselves and an introverted aspect. Both must be honored and given the time they require.

Gifts

The 4/1 has the gift of friendliness along with a curious and persuasive nature. They are taking in and learning about all of life, from the material to the relational level. They also tend to have uncanny street smarts. Acutely aware of what's going on around them, they can assess situations. With an innate strength, they can be the backbone of their network (friends, family, work, and spiritual community). They're not easily pushed around, which gives them a quality of being able to be counted on.

When I first came to Maui, I was introduced to the Ram Dass community. There were weekly swims with Ram Dass and weekly chanting sessions at his home in Haiku. Being around Ram Dass was magical. His loving presence emanated a deep ease and grace. The community around him were sweet and open. Many of my friends were close to Ram Dass and went to his home weekly. The trick was getting invited to those chanting sessions. You had to go through his right-hand person, Dassima, a 4/1 Profile. Dassi had that keen awareness of who to let in the circle. She was protective of Ram Dass. She was also acutely aware of the space limitations. Dassi created a sense of stability that Ram Dass and the community relied on. She was the perfect person to act in the guardian role.

I also have a close friend and colleague, Deborah Sudarsky, who is a 4/1. She wrote the bestselling books *Embrace Your Psychic Gifts: The Guide to Spiritual Awakening* and *Meet Your Guides: Embracing Your Angels, Archangels, and Ascended Masters.* Deborah and I do a weekly podcast show together, *Navigating Life Energies,* so I know her well. In her story, she was always connected to her guides, but her family had no context for her experience. She always felt different but didn't know why. When she discovered her 4/1 Profile, some pieces fit into place for her.

I love our friendship. I love doing the podcasts with Deborah. No matter how chaotic life is, she always has a core ground. She's one of those people who have gone their own way regardless of the cultural norm. For example, she grew up in a family of intellectuals and became a psychic. Then, as a Jewish woman, she was called to work at private Catholic high schools. When she discovered her deceased father was also a 4/1, Deborah understood him better as well. Like her, he was the backbone of the family. Deborah embodies the gift of an easy relational style with pragmatic smarts. She emanates ground, loyalty, and care. All qualities of the 4/1 Profile.

Challenges

The 4/1 faces a few challenges. For one, they can easily be misunderstood. Because they do not and cannot pretzel themselves to fit other people's expectations of them, they can be judged as rigid, inflexible, and unwilling to compromise. The truth is, they just are who they are. They may agree with you at a surface level, but underneath, they are not changing their ways. Because of their oak-tree-like quality, they can seem immovable. And that can be hard for people. As a result, the 4/1 can feel misunderstood, undervalued, and not seen. They are not willfully trying to be stubborn. In relationships, there is just not much give. There is a tension between being gregarious and friendly; wanting and needing relationships and community; and, at the same time, not being flexible in relationship. The 4/1 has little tolerance for people who don't go their way. They can be challenging to coach, especially if the coach (parent, therapist, or boss) is thinking their job is to help the 4/1 shift their stance. The person coaching a 4/1 must really work with them rather than trying to move them. The 4/1 will not abdicate their inner sensibility, but with clear, pragmatic information, the 4/1 can alter their direction.

While the 4/1 has this strong grounded quality, they also

have an insecurity. Both Line 1 and Line 4 have the challenge of gathering enough information to establish their sense of security and authority. Without the necessary information, they can flounder.

The 4/1 sees the world through a different lens than the rest of us and can become confused when people don't see what is obvious to them. They also can't tolerate people resisting them and will tend to let friendships fall away that don't align with their perspectives.

WORKING WITH A 4/1 PROFILE

You have a 4/1 client! In all my work with Human Design, I've looked at less than twenty people's charts who have a 4/1 Profile. They are rare and notable. Seeing that you or someone you know has this Profile is a big deal. They are truly unique from all the other Profiles. It's the equivalent of working with a Reflector in terms of how few there are. Be ready to work with them in a different way.

On the one hand, 4/1 Profiles present clear and straightforward. They are who they are. What you see is what you get. On the other hand, you may not really know what's going on underneath. They will agree with you on the surface to be nice without any intention of following your advice.

The key things to remember are not to resist them and not to try to change them.

Instead, listen to them. Be curious. Help them gather the information they need to understand themselves and others. This might seem like guidance you would give any coach when they're working with someone, but with the 4/1, it takes on another dimension. Trust that they will have the answers and help draw their answers out of them. When you do give input, be pragmatic with them. The 4/1 will respond to things that make sense to them. Just know that they're going to do things their way, even if it doesn't make sense to you.

While I've only encountered a limited number of 4/1s, they stand out. In fact, three were in my book writing business coaching program. I learned a lot about them by witnessing how they were coached and how they responded to coaching. I saw the 4/1's friendliness, their capacity to connect, and their engagement in the process. I also saw them struggle, at times coming to loggerheads with the coaching staff. As long as they were cherry picking what worked for them in the program, they were successful. But following the program hook, line, and sinker was like putting a square peg in a round hole. It just didn't work. You can never put a 4/1 Profile into a structure that's set. The structure must be created in relation to them.

Here are a few personal stories about my early experiences with people with a 4/1 Profile before I knew who they were or what a 4/1 was. Hopefully, they can give you a flavor of what not working well with a 4/1 looks like!

My wife and I had a niece, Rachel, who was a 4/1 Manifestor. We adored Rachel. She was special to us. She was definitely her own being and lived true to herself. The only girl in a family with four boys, she had a rough childhood story. When she was young, her father went to prison for abusing her. Things went downhill from there.

Wracked with physical pain, later diagnosed as fibromyalgia, she was swept into the opioid disaster. My wife and I felt protective of her. We invited her and her son to live on our property in rural Iowa. The impulse was an act of care on our part. We wanted to get her out of Florida and the network of friends that seemed less than optimal. We wanted to support her and help her heal. And yet, when I look back at our attempts to "help" her, I cringe.

We treated her as if we knew what would improve her life. We dropped her and her son into the Transcendental Meditation community that was totally foreign to her. We introduced her to new-age healing modalities and technologies. While our intentions were good, we were off track. Our lack of understanding kept us from authentically hearing her experience and needs. Remember, people with a 4/1 Profile are not shape shifters. They cannot alter themselves to fit situations. Situations and people must fit to them. Rachel tried valiantly, but it was a no go. Her story ended with an early death and a heavy heart on our part. Shortly after her death, I discovered she was a 4/1 Manifestor. How differently I would have approached her had I known.

Two of my close friends are 4/1 Profiles. Karla was part of Sukhasiddhi, my Tibetan Buddhist sangha in Marin. We met in 2004 at a Green Tara retreat, where we took refuge together. She was friendly, enthusiastic, and engaged. I liked Karla immediately. The only problem was, I was totally overwhelmed by her energy. It would be another ten years before I ran her Human Design chart and discovered she was a 4/1 Profile with eight Defined Centers.

In 2009, we traveled to India with a group from our sangha for a monthlong retreat to receive the Shangpa empowerments from Tai Situ Rinpoche. I had asked for a private room, but on the bus ride from New Delhi to the Tibetan Center in Himachal Pradesh, I found out I was paired to room with Karla. It's not pretty when a grown woman traveling on a spiritual pilgrimage has a full-on temper tantrum and acts like a three year old, which is what I did. I was outraged. I was terrified. I had suffered a concussion in 2006 with a slow recovery. This was my first foray into travel and being in out-of-control situations. It was not going well. We got to our room, and it had mold. Another assault on my oversensitive system. In my fury and terror, I shut down. I couldn't even look at Karla, much less talk to her or relate to her. I was horrible. I got up at four in the morning and did my movement lessons and meditations. I felt bombarded. I needed to calm my nervous system and connect to myself. At this point, the whole thing is somewhat of a blur. I know I raged at her. I blamed her. I was a mess, trying desperately to be safe in what felt like a very unsafe situation.

Karla didn't budge. She remained friendly, kind, and loving towards me. She was curious and open. She wanted to hear my experience. She wanted to understand her impact on me. She listened. I was shocked. Her ground, her stability, and her openness allowed me the safety to relax and unwind, to see myself, and to recognize her care.

When I talk to other people with a 4/1 Profile, I hear a similar story. They are the ground for people. They are curious. They can tolerate people's craziness. One colleague told me it was easy to be nonjudgmental. She doesn't struggle with judgements the way she sees other people struggle.

On that trip, Karla and I bonded. I was impacted by her ability to stand strong and stay connected in the middle of my meltdown. Even now, as I remember that trip, I am touched by her love and care. I am in awe by the capacity of the 4/1 to stand their ground in the face of adversity.

As our lives unfolded, we shared many adventures, mostly in the realm of meditation and healing. I loved and appreciated her, but some part of me still thought I had to help her with her struggles. Once I ran her chart and discovered she was a 4/1 with eight Defined Centers, something clicked. I understood her at a whole new level. I stopped seeing her struggles as calls for help and started seeing her from an expanded perspective.

GUIDED MEDITATION

Imagine for a moment that you are a unique, once-in-a-lifetime being brought to Earth with a particular mission. You have an important purpose. What you have to bring is invaluable to the larger puzzle of humanity. Your light cannot be replicated by anyone else.

To ignite your purpose and ensure that your light is turned on, you've been given a gift: your Profile. You have been gifted the 4/1 Profile. This Profile gives you insight into how to realize your potential. It shows you the mechanism or the learning style that will call forth your purpose.

Take a moment to put everything aside and come to the present moment.
Allow your awareness to shift from ordinary consciousness to extraordinary consciousness.
Begin by connecting with your body.
Sense your arms and legs.
Sense your belly center.
Take a breath.
Settle into the awareness of your entire body.
Now, shift your awareness to your 4/1 Profile.
Feel the friendliness of your Conscious 4th Line.
The aspect of you that likes to connect with people.
The part of you that is curious about people.
That cares about people.
Now, connect with the Unconscious 1st Line.
Here you are curious about the world and everything in it.
What fascinates you?
What do you want to study or learn?
Do you know?
Can you appreciate your ravenous curiosity?
Now feel the energies of your Conscious Line 4 and your Unconscious Line 1 in harmony.
Your active wonder.
Are you aware you are different from most other people?
How?
Are you the backbone of your family or your community?

Shel Silverstein was a 4/1. He wrote the Giving Tree.
Are you like that Giving Tree?
Take a moment to appreciate yourself.
Know that even if people don't understand you, you're
    going to do what you know to do.
Feel your strength.
Feel your connection to people.
Stand in your glory.
Smile at your 4/1 Profile.
Ask it if it has any guidance for you.
Thank it.
Be still with yourself.
When you're ready, gently bring your awareness back to
    the room.
Sense your arms and legs.
Sense your belly center.
Take a moment to reflect on what arose.
If you're called, journal to anchor your thoughts.

Note: *If you want an audio recording of this meditation, reach out to me with your Profile details at info@clientsandhumandesign.com.*

13

THE 5/1 PROFILE

HERETIC/INVESTIGATOR

Themes

• Most transpersonal with the highest universalizing potential

• Projected on (positively and negatively)

• Seductive/hidden

• Insecurities and vulnerabilities

• Here to lead in crisis with practical solutions

• Karmic relationships

• Here to impact strangers of consequence

Entelechy: *True alchemists, this extraordinary Profile takes knowledge they have garnered and transmutes it, bringing high-level practical solutions that serve all humanity.*

Famous 5/1 Profiles

Madonna, Ellen DeGeneres, Queen Elizabeth, Angela Merkel, Reese Witherspoon, Mary Tyler Moore, Troy Aikman, Louis Armstrong, Neil Armstrong, Richard Bach, Joan Baez, Holly Near, Anne Frank, Buckminster Fuller, Ken Wilber, Paul McCartney, Theo Van Gogh, Ra Uru Hu, Tina Turner, Toni Morrison, Frida Kahlo, Yo Yo Ma, Hazrat Inayat Kahn, Martin Luther King Jr.

Overview

This potent combination is the most transpersonal of the 12 Profiles. Here, Line 1's quest for knowledge mixes with Line 5's capacity to save humanity. In this marriage, new mutative solutions are born.

The 5/1 is hungry for knowledge. They then take that knowledge and transform it, making it usable at a higher level. This has far-reaching and universal implications.

With a seductive nature, they draw people towards them. Meanwhile, people sense that the 5/1 has some capacity or some information that will support them. Waiting to be called into service, the 5/1 must discern what is a good call and if the timing is right. They fulfill their dharma when they respond to calls that are in alignment with their Strategy and Authority. In this scenario, they have done their investigative homework and bring practical solutions that work. If the 5/1 leaps to help without honoring their Strategy and Authority and without having done their investigative work, they are unable to provide the solution needed. In this scenario, the projection field flips, and they fall from grace. Where they were first drawn in, they are now spewed out. Thus, they are either heralded or disgraced.

Living in a projection field, the 5/1 hides out. They only reveal themselves to a few trustworthy people. Their relationships are karmic, and they are here to impact strangers.

THE CONSCIOUS LINE 5

The Heretic (The Illuminator)

The Conscious 5th Line is considered the highest line of the Hexagram. With a Line 5 in the Profile the whole chart is taken to a universal level. The 5th Lines have a big responsibility. They are here to serve humanity with their influential power and capacity to solve problems. How they go about doing that will depend on which line the 5th Line is paired with. Here, paired with Line 1, answers become clear through research.

Regardless of how the 5th Line resolves crises, they are recognized by others as someone who has the capacity to help. They are sought out and called upon. They also call others to them. With a seductive and magnetic pull, they attract the people they are to serve.

The 5th Line is projected on. They are not seen for who they are but rather for who people want them to be. They act as mirrors, showing people what they need to heal in themselves. If the 5th Line is in the wrong place at the wrong time getting or responding to the wrong projections, they can be the object of negative projections. This can be hard for the Line 5, especially if they take the projections personally.

If the 5th Line is getting positive projections but then believes the projections to be personally about them, they can get entwined in believing they *are* the savior rather than the bringers of the solution. As important as it is for the 5th Line to come up with practical solutions, it is equally important that they know when to step away. If the 5th Line stays too long, the positive projection can turn negative. Likewise, if the 5th Line's solution doesn't work, they can be negatively projected on.

The 5th Line has a natural leadership and broad, influential reach. Its name, "Heretic," points to the 5th Line's challenge of being negatively projected on as they bring new solutions to humanity that may or may not be received or work.

Line 5 is here to impact strangers of consequence rather than people who they already know. This is the Profile of someone who has karmic relationships. Every meeting with a stranger is potentially life changing.

THE UNCONSCIOUS LINE 1

The Investigator

The 1st Line has an element of insecurity which is remedied by gaining information. People with a Line 1 in their Profile need to know all they can. Information nourishes them. It puts them at ease. They are designed to be drawn to what interests them and relish in the learning process. Through study, they gain knowledge. As they become experts and share their knowledge, they bring a new level of stability to others. The 1st Lines are here to create a solid foundation for all of us. In order to do that, they need alone time.

THE 5/1 PROFILE

When we combine the Conscious 5th Line and the Unconscious 1st Line something extraordinary happens. In this alchemical meeting, mutative knowledge becomes the source of new solutions for humanity. The 1st Line has a voracious appetite for knowledge. Out of an insecurity, and a need to create a foundation, they become absorbed in learning things that interest them. It seems very personal, in service of the self, at that 1st Line level. But as the knowledge connects with the 5th Line, everything changes. No longer personal, the knowledge expands to encompass a larger universal domain. There's a powerful transmutation that serves humanity.

This dynamic alchemical process is compelling and draws others to the 5/1. People sense that the 5/1 has something of value to offer or something they need. They project onto the 5/1 the role of savior.

There is a seductive quality – an air of possibility that surrounds the 5/1. Meanwhile, the 5/1 feels the pressure to be a savior. They may not understand it, and they may question it. But they know they are here to make a difference. They know they have something the world needs.

The 5/1 Profile is the first of the four Left Angle Crosses. Unlike the Right Angle Crosses, which have a Personal Destiny, this group has a Transpersonal Destiny. Here, the 5/1 is processing and understanding their life through their interactions with others. Each meeting is said to be karmic. You could think of it as a prior agreement to meet in this lifetime. Each encounter is potentially life changing for all involved. Thus, interactions with people carry extra weight and importance for those with a Left Angle Cross.

Gifts

The 5/1 has the huge gift of being the saviors of humanity. With their ravenous curiosity and capacity to absorb knowledge, they gather an information base that becomes the foundation of the new order. They have the enviable gift of bringing practical solutions to seemingly unsolvable problems. With their seductive nature they can draw people to them to transform the world.

Denise Anderson has a 5/1 Profile. She is a colleague, a best-selling author, and certified Human Design Consultant and Practitioner. Denise epitomizes the gifts of the 5/1 Profile. In her presence, you feel a sparkle in the air. She has something – something magnificent. Her blazing curiosity awakens the field. She is gathering information about life and bringing new ways to meet it. Her work with elders in a retirement community in Canada is transforming how they approach the last years of their lives. Among other things, Denise is bringing a new solution to aging.

Challenges

With all the glory inherent in the 5/1 offerings, there are challenges here as well. How do they navigate with this huge gift? If they are at all off track, the consequences are huge.

We've talked about how the 5th Line is projected on. Talk to any 5/1 and you will hear stories of how they had to weather some fall from grace and where they had to repair their image. This is an ongoing concern for the 5/1.

Think about Ellen Degeneres, who, early on in her career, was the darling with her own show. In 1997, after four successful seasons of the sitcom *Ellen*, she came out as gay. Initially her ratings skyrocketed only to plummet in the fifth season. As a result, the show was cancelled. Acting as the Heretic, she messed with society's image of a straight world. Ultimately, she ushered in a new order, which included gays and lesbians becoming prominent on television. More recently, Ellen admitted to being boxed in by her overly nice reputation. When employees went public about harassment and a toxic workplace, Ellen had to publicly address the issues. Her image took a hit.

Or look at Reese Witherspoon, who is known for her *Legally Blonde*, bubbly, innocent, perfect image. In 2013, her husband was pulled over for suspicion of driving under the influence. Reese apparently got a bit belligerent with the officer and was arrested for obstruction of justice. Her image took a hit, and she had to do damage repair. She made public apologies for her behavior.

Another example of a 5/1 having to manage hits to her image is Queen Elizabeth. She came up with the "wrong" solution when she responded to Princess Diana's death. She believed the "problem" would be forgotten after a few days. When the outpouring for Diana grew in unprecedented ways, The Queen's silence became an embarrassment. We could say she didn't do her research. She was out of touch with the impact of the public sentiment. Her image took a hit. She had to pivot her PR stance to one of embracing Diana.

The fall from grace can happen in a variety of scenarios. Trouble ensues if the 5/1 responds to the wrong call or does so in the wrong timing or if the 5/1 hasn't done their homework and doesn't come up with a practical solution. Likewise, if they stay too long in a situation, their reputation can be damaged.

Not knowing when to extricate themselves, the challenge of when to leave is a very real one for people with a 5/1 profile. Many of my 5th Line clients and students talk about their experience of stepping into situations in response to a call. They showed up for the task at hand and had a noteworthy impact for companies or organizations. They were praised – even seen as heroes. Then, as time went on, something shifted. They were no longer needed. It's as if they became a problem rather than the solution.

This potential fall messes with the mindset of the 5/1. After all, their intentions are good. They want to be helpful. They're often left not knowing what went wrong.

Positive projections can be equally challenging for this Profile. People can feel very strongly that the 5/1 is the savior. Is it true? How long will the projection last? If the 5/1's ego gets wrapped in the projection, they can believe they're someone in a puffed-up way. The 5/1 must learn to take a very mature and somewhat detached stance. The challenge is to see the projections for what they are.

Line 1 challenges arise if they are not given or do not take the time to be in their own world absorbed in learning. They need this time in order to deepen their knowledge base. Without this, they do not have the practical solutions needed to support Line 5.

WORKING WITH A 5/1 PROFILE

When you have a client with a 5/1 Profile, there are a number of things to consider. First, be clear who you are working with. This person has enormous capacity to impact the world. You have to navigate the fine line of seeing their potential without getting lost in a positive projection. Be aware of your own hopes, wishes, and desires for the person that may have nothing to do with them.

Here's an example of a recent time when I fell into this trap. My 5/1 nephew Travis has spent the last twenty years rafting rivers in China. It began when he accompanied his dad, my brother Pete, on first descent river expeditions in China and Tibet. After getting a degree in Chinese, Travis started a river rafting company in China. A lover of nature, his intent was to educate the Chinese about the healing power of nature. He wanted to raise awareness in the Chinese to protect their rivers, which he has done.

Now, Travis is living in Montana with his four-year-old daughter and assessing what's next. After sharing his chart with him, I suggested he check out NARM (Neuro Affective Relational Model). NARM is an exceptional training for coaches, therapists, and healers that works with relational trauma and the process of healing by reconnecting with our innate urges.

Travis was deeply impacted by his experience with NARM. He said it was the closest thing to being on the river in that suspended time/space opening of authentic being. Wanting to run some thoughts by me, he reached out. Travis wanted to bring NARM to the world. He explained that he wanted to introduce NARM to places like the National Park Service. He wanted to bring it to people on river trips. Of course, he did! This is a perfect example of Line 1 taking the information to Line 5, bringing a solution to the isolation and despair humans feel as a result of being cut off from our natural beingness.

Travis wasn't clear if he should get a degree in social work so he could continue his NARM studies and be more legit. Because he is a Generator, I asked him some sacral yes/no questions to help him get more information. That was good on my part. Meanwhile, I had my very strong opinions and preferences! I projected who I thought he should be on to him. I saw where he was going and what a transformational impact he could have. I was clear. He should get his PhD. He would get bogged down in social work. His path was bigger.

I tried to sell him on the idea as if it were the final truth. But it was my image for him – my desire. I stopped listening to him. After we got off the call, I knew I had projected on to him. I needed to go back and clean that up.

So, as a coach or therapist or boss, just be aware of the tendency to project your needs and desires on to 5th Lines! Share with your client the power of the 5/1 Profile. Let them know they have a dharma to save the world. Often, they'll tell you it's a relief to know that. It's something they've felt driven by but haven't understood. Help them understand the projection field they inhabit and name the challenges they face with it.

My 5/1 friend, certified Human Design consultant and practitioner, colleague, and bestselling author Kristin Panek works with leaders. She mastered her relationship with the projection field when she entered a mystery school. There, she was guided to deliberately take on the role of being projected on. While people did their shadow work, she would be the placeholder of the mother, the wife, and the child of whomever was working. This was an ingenious way to understand and get comfortable with the projection field.

Work with the 5/1 to help them recognize what constitutes a good calling and what it means to wait for right timing. Their Type, Strategy, and Authority will be invaluable here. Help your client understand the inherent challenges they'll encounter if they don't respond to a calling from an aligned place. Support them to indulge in their learning process. To honor their pull to learn, knowing it will serve them when the time comes. Explain that they'll do best if they first solve a problem then hand it over. Give them permission to not stick around to complete the project.

Reflect their role as someone to impact strangers. Their relationships are karmic. They never know who will offer the opportunity for them to realize their dharma. Point out that they may not be as successful with the people close to them and familiar to them as they are with people they know less well.

Above all, appreciate the yoke they carry and responsibility that comes with it.

GUIDED MEDITATION

Imagine for a moment that you are a unique, once-in-a-lifetime being brought to Earth with a particular mission. You have an important purpose. You are bringing an invaluable piece to the larger puzzle of humanity. Your light cannot be replicated by anyone else.

To ignite your purpose and ensure that your light is turned on, you've been given a gift: your Profile. You have been gifted the 5/1 Profile. This Profile gives you insight into how to realize your potential. It shows you the mechanism or the learning style that will call forth your purpose.

*Take a moment to pause and connect with your 5/1
    Profile.*

Put everything aside.

Let the past fall away.

Let the future dissipate.

Turn your attention to the present moment.

*Allow your awareness to shift from ordinary consciousness
    to extraordinary consciousness.*

Begin by connecting with your body.

Sense your arms and legs.

Sense your belly center.

Take a breath.

Settle into the awareness of your entire body.

Now, call your 5/1 Profile into your awareness.

Connect with it.

Open to the gifts it brings.

*Feel the desire of your Conscious 5th Line to serve
    humanity.*

*Feel the pull of your Unconscious 1st Line to acquire
    knowledge.*

Recognize its voracious appetite.

*Can you allow yourself to surrender to the desire to gather
    information?*

The need for it?

*Can you give yourself the time you need to be absorbed in
    learning?*

*Do you recognize that this knowledge is bigger than your
    personal desire to understand?*

*That you will be called to take it to the world to solve
    problems?*

That you will be called to transform humanity?

It's a big job.

*Your world is complicated by the fact that people do not
    really see you.*

They see that you can help them. They want that help.
But are you the person for that particular job?
Can you listen?
Someone, some situation, needs what you know and needs
  what you have to offer.
Can you imagine waiting for the right time and the right
  call?
Can you imagine stepping out and offering your practical,
  transformational solutions?
Notice as people tell stories about you.
They are projecting on you.
Can you let them?
Can you see they are using you as a mirror?
Their stories have nothing to do with you.
Not the positive ones, where they put you on a pedestal
  and sing your praises.
Not the negative ones, where they trash you in their disap-
  pointment.
Can you let the projections pass you by?
Can you remember what you are here to do?
Can you honor your role?
Can you stand in the awareness that your knowledge is
  needed?
Humanity awaits you.
Take a moment as you connect with the energy of the 5/1
  Profile.
See if it would be ok to ask it for guidance.
What do you need to do to align more deeply with this
  powerful force?
What wisdom does it have for you?
Thank it.
And then bring your awareness back to your body.
Sense your arms and legs.
Breathe into your belly center.

Be still.
Let your awareness of your 5/1 energy incubate.
Now, take time to anchor your experience by journaling
   your takeaways.

Note: If you want an audio recording of this meditation, reach out to
me with your Profile details at info@clientsandhumandesign.com.

14

THE 5/2 PROFILE

HERETIC/HERMIT

Themes

• Luminaries

• Don't like being or feeling pressured

• Challenge to know what the right call to respond to is

• Deeply gifted, yet vulnerable to accessing and bringing their gifts into the world

• Need to come out in their own timing in their own way

• Even so, they can be reluctant to step out

• Projected on (positively and negatively)

• Here to impact strangers of consequence

Entelechy: This rare and deeply gifted Profile has the powerful potential to bring forth innovative revelations that both impact the world and nourish themselves.

Famous 5/2 Profiles

Alvin Ailey, Justin Bieber, Robert De Niro, Tommy Hilfiger, Loreena McKennitt, Caroline Myss, Dick Van Dyke, Abraham Lincoln, George Eliot, Mike Wallace, Franz Shubert, Marlon Brando, Holly Near

Overview

The Conscious 5th Line and the Unconscious 2nd Line are in a harmonic. Both are attracting people's projections. Line 2 wants to be left alone, but the Line 5 is pulled by their feeling of karmic duty to help people. However, the 5/2 profile can question their capacity to fulfill that duty, so they can tend to hang back and remain disengaged. This is a loss for everyone.

Unpressured alone time is the golden key for the 5/2 Profile. This enables them to access themselves and the bounty of riches that lie in wait deep within. In this unpressured state, they listen for the right inner call that can engage their gifts and transform the world. Even with the unpressured alone time, accessing their gifts is the great challenge. They have the unusual vulnerability of having to recognize and source those hidden talents on their own followed by the challenge of having to take a stand for them before their gifts are recognized by others.

THE CONSCIOUS LINE 5

The Heretic (The Illuminator)

Line 5 is understood to be the highest line of the Hexagram. With a 5th Line in the Profile the whole chart shifts from a personal level to a universal level. The person with a 5th Line is in service to humanity. They are designed to bring new and practical solutions to the world.

5th Lines rely on their seductive magnetism to draw the people to them who need their gifts. Positively projected on, they are seen and recognized as someone who has the capacity to help. People also seek out 5th Lines and expect them to come up with answers to their problems. When the Line 5 comes through with practical solutions, they are heralded as saviors. If the 5th Line fails to come up with a workable solution, they are negatively projected on, and their reputation suffers. Because the 5th Line is operating at a broader, universal level, the damage to their reputation can be far reaching.

THE UNCONSCIOUS LINE 2

The Hermit

The Unconscious Line 2 has a quality of insecurity. People with this line have a special gift and a unique genius. This is an innate talent that doesn't require study. The only problem is, the 2nd Line is only vaguely aware of their hidden capacities. They have no idea how to articulate or share their distinctive brilliance – thus, the insecurity. In most cases, we say that when the 2nd Line is *hermitting* – puttering in their own world, doing what they love – other people see them and call them out. Their innate talent is recognized as something extraordinary. In the case of the 5/2 Profile, they aren't called out by another. They must recognize a call within themselves. It is in their downtime, when they are free of pressure, that they perceive a call that will give them the opening to share their hidden treasures. To access their 2nd Line gifts, they must follow their Type, Strategy, and Authority, or else they risk not bringing them forth.

THE 5/2 PROFILE

With a Conscious Line 5 and an Unconscious Line 2, the 5/2 Profile lives in a double projection field. We could say that the projections for this type are even more potent than for the other 5th Lines. They rely on projections and are waiting for the right projections that will activate their energy to bring forth their talents. At the same time, they are having to continuously sort through projections because the 5th Line is not here to help everyone in crisis, nor are they designed to offer help continuously.

As I look at the list of people I know or have worked with who have a 5/2 Profile, I am aware of a certain quality of solidity and strength along with an elusiveness. They are all remarkable, yet there is a hidden quality. They have a mystery about them. Something that is hard to grasp. Once they access themselves, it's almost as if they pop, and their gifts pour forth.

With an innate capacity or genius, the 5/2 is sought after for their expertise. In the 1980s, Caroline Myss lectured in Berkeley, California, where I was living. She brought a revolutionary view of health and healing. She talked about the connection of unresolved emotions and illness. She introduced the concept of suffering as currency. She described the propensity to gather and share our woes as a way to connect. Her compelling story of discovering she was a medical intuitive awakened a new possibility for many. Her innate gift was sought after by Norman Shealy, founder of the American Holistic Health Association, and the likes of Oprah Winfrey, who had her on her show multiple times. Caroline became the voice of medical intuition as she became a popular speaker, workshop leader, and author.

Eventually, she established a school to train people to develop their intuition. Caroline is an example of recognizing her internal gifts and bringing forth new solutions for humanity.

The 5/2 Profile is one of the rarer profiles. What they have to bring is astounding but finding the pathway to bring it out from the depths can be challenging. First, it's hard for them to know what they're bringing. Then, it's hard to know if the calling is correct. They must stand in faith, trusting themselves while they convince others that their treasure is indeed worthy. All the while they're not exactly sure themselves that they can have the impact or bring the solution that is called for. There is a hidden quality to this Profile; both the 5 and the 2 are a bit undercover. Alvin Ailey, who was bold and brilliant in his dance choreography, kept the fact that he was gay hidden. At his death from AIDS-related illness, he asked the doctor to announce that his death was from a terminal blood disease in order to protect his mother from stigma.

Like the 5/1, the 5/2 Profile is one of the Left Angle Crosses. This group has a Transpersonal Destiny rather than a Personal Destiny. The 5/2 is unique in that it is working out its destiny karma in relationship to its past.

Gifts

It's actually a bit tricky to put words to the gifts of the 5/2. How do you describe the gifts of an orchid or the sunrise? People with a 5/2 Profile are like forces of nature. Once they recognize their gifts and bring them out to the world, they show up big across the sky. Their contribution is revolutionary, authentic, and natural. They can lead people to new dimensions. Their service becomes a selfless and generous outpouring of their very being. As they nourish others, they are themselves nourished.

Challenges

There are a few challenges that the 5/2 Profile faces. The first revolves around navigating their Unconscious Line 2. If they are not aware of their gifts, they can be caught in the 5th Line activity of saving the world before they have the support of their gifts to help them out.

They can also become pulled into the *hermit* vortex as a desperate attempt to protect themselves from the world and its pressures. If they don't know how to communicate their healthy need for space and time, they can put up a wall that gives the message to stay away. This can be experienced as rejection and be confusing in relationships.

That Line 2 is the doorway for the 5/2. They have the challenge of taking the time necessary to *hermit* followed by the challenge of recognizing their gift while they are in that *hermit* environment. (Remember, they aren't seen and called out by others in the same way that other Line 2s are.)

Once they recognize their gifts, they have the challenge of waiting for the call to bring them forth. Once they get a call, they must use their Strategy and Authority to recognize if it's the right call in the right timing. Once they answer the call, they have to stand in their belief in the solution they're bringing as their Line 5 brings those gifts out into the world. This must happen even before anyone else recognizes them.

Whew. All that before even discussing the challenge of being projected on.

So, let's talk about that.

Both the 5th Line and the 2nd Line are projected on big time.

The 5/2 has the challenge of stepping out to save the world, not answering the right call, not coming through with what people expect of them, and having their reputation trashed. Remember, the 5th Line impacts a large world, so the reputation crash can be daunting. If the projections are negative the 5/2 can go deeper into hiding. The challenge of coming out behind the veil can be exacerbated. The 5/2 has a lot to navigate here.

WORKING WITH A 5/2 PROFILE

First and foremost, you have to realize you're working with a very special person who has a big job that they may not be sure if they can follow through on. They are under pressure within themselves to figure out when and how to help. Your task is hold how amazing they are. Recognize that it may be a process for them to access their hidden gifts and bring them out in the world.

You are going to want to address the need for *hermit* time to access their riches. Help them look at that Line 2. Are they honoring it? Are they using it defensively to hide?

Whatever you do, don't pressure them. That can easily push them back into their hidden safe haven. Let them come out in their own timing. Help them get clear on their relationship to pressure. How do they respond to it?

If you come across a 5/2 Profile who is a pressure junkie, you might look to see if they have an Open Root. They may be conditioned to operate on adrenalized energy. They may not yet know that they have a treasure waiting for them if they can slow down and allow themselves to take their *hermit* time.

Maha took our Human Design Certification Training for Professionals and said that discovering her 5/2 Profile was the biggest awakening of all the layers. It was huge for her. There was so much confusion around the seeming polarities inside of her that she couldn't seem to reconcile. For example, was she an introvert or an extrovert? Her 5th Line had an extroverted quality, while her 2nd Line was shy.

She felt shame and embarrassment around her 2nd Line. She said, "Never in a million years did I imagine the Line 2 space was productive or fertile or that real work was happening there.

The 5/2 Profile helped me understand the value of the work of rest..."

Maha is a Manifesting Generator with an Open Root Center. We might think that another Human Design Type might have a different experience. But I wonder if that Unconscious Line 2 is tricky for all 5/2 Profiles to access.

Linda is a successful business coach. She's also a Projector – again, with an Open Root. Before she learned Human Design, she was a lot like Maha: crazy busy. She ran circles around me. Once she understood her Projector Type and her Profile, she made a radical shift. She began to deeply honor her need for space and downtime. She actually ended up being less stressed and more successful as a result.

For both Linda and Maha, the reflection that they were being projected on had a big impact. It helped put things in perspective. For Maha, it was a major aha. From a young age, she understood that people had extreme reactions to her, either despising her or loving her with nothing in between. She knew their feelings bore no relationship to her. Meanwhile, her 5th Line would show up with solutions that would shock and rattle people. She described herself crashing and, like a vampire, needing to hide from the daylight.

Linda now knows that she is like a blank slate that people project on. People don't see her. She's learned to let it go. She only lets her screen down with a few people who are really present with her. Otherwise, she says that when people are projecting there is nothing she can do, and she watches as her screen thickens.

My sister's husband, Jean, has a 5/2 Profile. Heidi describes him going into his man cave and hiding. She realizes when she pressures him, he goes further in and becomes inaccessible. As Heidi became clear that Jean's *hermit* time is deeply nourishing for him, she shifted her approach.

Jean is an interesting case because he spent thirty-five years as a translator, in a high-pressure deadline job that took from him. When he was introduced to NARM (Neuro Affective Relational Model), he learned to access his desires; his urges; and, we could say, his gifts. At sixty-eight, he found a life he never imagined possible. He now gives NARM sessions to people to help them connect to themselves. He recognized his gifts, heard the call, and is living a life in aligned service.

GUIDED MEDITATION

Imagine for a moment that you are a unique, once-in-a-lifetime being brought to earth with a particular mission. You have an important purpose. You have an invaluable gift you're bringing to the larger puzzle of humanity. Your light cannot be replicated by anyone else.

To ignite your purpose and ensure that your light is turned on, you have been gifted with the 5/2 Profile. This Profile offers insight into how to realize your potential. It shows you the mechanism or the learning style that will call forth your purpose.

> *Take a moment to pause and connect with your 5/2*
> > *Profile.*
> *Put everything aside.*
> *Let the past fall away.*
> *Forget about the future.*
> *Turn your attention to the present moment.*
> *Allow your awareness to shift from ordinary consciousness*
> > *to extraordinary consciousness.*
> *Begin by connecting with your body.*
> *Sense your arms and legs.*
> *Sense your belly center.*
> *Take a breath.*
> *Settle into the awareness of your entire body.*

Now, call your 5/2 Profile into your awareness.

Connect with it.

Open to the gifts it brings.

Sense your Conscious Line 5.

The part of you that is ready to serve humanity.

Line 5 is waiting for a calling.

It knows it has a big responsibility to solve problems.

And yet it is reluctant.

Unsure.

Can it come through?

Feel the desire of your Unconscious 2nd Line to be alone.

The urge to be in your own space.

Can you allow yourself to go there?

Can you give yourself time with you?

*When you're there, can you allow yourself to recognize
    your unique gifts?*

Perhaps stand in awe of them.

Listen and wait.

*Someone, some situation, needs what you especially have
    to offer.*

*Can you imagine waiting for the right time and the right
    call?*

*Can you imagine stepping out and offering your magnifi-
    cent greatness to the world?*

Notice as people tell stories about you.

They are projecting on you.

Can you let them?

Can you see they are using you as a mirror?

Their stories have nothing to do with you.

*Not the positive ones, where they put you on a pedestal
    and sing your praises.*

*Not the negative ones, where they trash you in their disap-
    pointment.*

Can you let the projections pass you by?

Can you remember who you are?

Can you cherish who you are?

Can you stand in the awareness that your gifts are needed treasures?

Humanity awaits you.

Take a moment and connect more deeply with the energy of the 5/2 Profile.

See if it would be OK to ask it for guidance.

What do you need to do to align more deeply with this powerful force?

What wisdom does it have for you?

Thank it.

And then bring your awareness back to your body.

Sense your arms and legs.

Breathe into your belly center.

Be still.

Let your awareness of your 5/2 energy incubate.

Now, take time to anchor your experience by journaling your takeaways.

Note: If you want an audio recording of this meditation, reach out to me with your Profile details at info@clientsandhumandesign.com.

15

THE 6/2 PROFILE

ROLE MODEL/HERMIT

Themes

- Triphasic

- Detached

- Old souls, wise guides

- Perfectionists

- Trust is crucial

- Unique gifts must be called out

- Looking for soulmate

- Here to impact strangers of consequence

Entelechy: The 6/2 Profiles carry the gift of wisdom. These old souls bring the capacity to live their truth from an internal authority. Acting as role models, they show humanity an alternative to the propensity to abandon oneself for an outer authority.

Famous 6/2 Profiles

Maya Angelo, Michelle Obama, Barack Obama, Charles de Gaulle, Charles Dickens, George Lucas, Isadora Duncan, Harry Truman, Ammachi, Tony Robbins, Neale Donald Walsch, Pablo Neruda, Elton John, Bruce Lee, Marilyn Monroe, Jamie Lee Curtis, Emily Brontë, Mahatma Gandhi

Overview

The 6/2 is a wise guide. With the Conscious 6th Line, they are looking at the big picture of life. With their Unconscious 2nd Line, they need to *hermit* in order to access their genius. Combining these two energies can give the 6/2 a detached quality. Designed to find their soulmates, they are optimists with a love of truth and a desire for perfection. The 6/2 Profiles look to their internal authority for guidance and become *role models* for what it means to live authentic lives. With their triphasic journey they have a theme of maturing over time.

Triphasic

The 6th Line has a triphasic journey:

• The first thirty years, they operate like 3rd Lines, learning by trial and error. During this phase, they are experimenting in order to discover what does and does not work. This can look like a series of "mistakes" as they gain firsthand knowledge about life. These "learnings" are an integral part of their process as they gather wisdom on the road to becoming the *Role Model*.

• From age thirty to fifty, the 6th Line then shifts its style of learning. No longer throwing themselves into the fire by experimenting, they step back to learn by becoming the observer. From this vantage, they gain perspective on life. Through witnessing life, they are generating information from a distance in order to deepen their wisdom and clarity.

• At their Kiron Return around age fifty and until their death, they are now in a position to live as the Role Model. However, to fully embody and bring their wisdom as the Role Model to fruition, they must embrace and integrate what they've learned through the experimentation and observation phases.

Regardless of the phase, the 6/2 Profile is often recognized as a wise being and emanates a transformational quality throughout their lives.

THE CONSCIOUS LINE 6

The Role Model

The Conscious Line 6 brings the wisdom of an old soul. It has a long view of life that can look ahead and see things that aren't yet accessible to others. This discrepancy can be unnerving for the 6th Line and make them doubt what they know. When the 6th Line recognizes their innate knowing, they can recalibrate to trust what they see and bring compassion to those who do not have their vantage.

The 6th Line is here to show humanity the possibility of living authentically by turning to an internal authority rather than relying on an external authority for guidance. They are optimistic seekers of truth who are looking for perfection in life.

Trust is an important theme for them, and they are in search of their soulmate.

Naturally detached, the 6th Line stands back as the witness, especially after the age of 30. They tend to stay on the edge of a group rather than immersing themselves in the middle of a group.

THE UNCONSCIOUS LINE 2

The Hermit

The Unconscious 2nd Line lives in a world of their own. They operate best when they have the time and space to follow their inclinations and see what unfolds. Their innate talent requires time alone without intrusions. In this context, the natural gifts of the 2nd Line are revealed, seen, and called out by others.

The Line 2 Profile tends to be slightly insecure and actually gets a sense of ground by being on their own and doing what they love. While they may sense that they have gifts, they are not necessarily clear what those gifts are or how to share them. These natural capacities are innate. They have a genius – a life calling that is waiting to be brought forth. But without the means to articulate what their gifts are or a clear understanding how they do what they do, they can remain in doubt. It takes others to bring them out into the world.

THE 6/2 PROFILE

When we look at the Conscious Line 6 and Unconscious Line 2 together, we see a person who is at once looking at the big picture and, at the same time, called to be in their own domain, doing their own thing. There is a detached quality with the 6th Line and a hidden quality with the 2nd Line, which makes for an interesting dynamic – a kind of introverted inclination that's looking outward at the larger view. The combination of these two profile energies gives a powerful democratic leadership element with a potent breadth and depth of wisdom.

There are a few things to consider with the 6/2 Profile. First, they are here to impact strangers of consequence – people they meet in the course of their life. Like the 5th Line, we say that every person the 6th Line encounters is a fated meeting. Every person brings either learning to enrich the 6th Line's wisdom or an opportunity for the 6th Line to share their wisdom. Each person could call out their gifts or be a recipient of them.

Take Mahatma Gandhi who has a 6/2 Profile. His story follows the triphasic life cycle of learning by trial and error for the first thirty years of his life. He was married at 13 to his 14-year-old wife. At 17, he had his first child. He dropped out of college after less than 6 months and at age 18, he left his wife to study in London. There he met became involved with the London Vegetarian Society where he was introduced to members of the Theosophical Society. He returned to India at 22 to discover his mother had died. Distressed by her passing, he was unable to cross examine witnesses so "failed" at starting a successful law practice. At 23, he moved to South Africa for 21 years. Here he raised a family and became involved in non-violent resistance as he campaigned for civil rights. His personal experience of being bullied in South Africa due to his skin color activated a desire to fight for the rights of those who are mistreated. At 45, he returned to India and began organizing farmers and laborers to protest against unfair land-tax and discrimination. Are you seeing how he is impacted by and impacting strangers?

At 52, as he stepped into his Role Model, he became a leader in the Indian National Congress. Here he campaigned nation-wide to ease poverty, expand women's rights, work for amenable religious and ethnic relations, and to establish self-rule. Gandhi is famous for leading the people of India to challenge the British-imposed salt tax, and demanding that the British leave

India. His influence as a leader who followed his inner authority continues to impact people far and wide to this day.

The second thing to consider is that the 6/2 Profile is looking for their soulmate. They may not feel settled until they find the person they are looking for. This can become a life's mission. I've had clients with a 6/2 Profiles suffer deeply when a person they thought was their soulmate left them. In this case the 6/2 can feel lost and without purpose. Regardless how well the rest of their life may be going, the pull to find *The One* can haunt them.

And third, trust measures high on the list of what's important for a 6/2 Profile. The capacity to be intimate will be almost impossible without a foundation of trust. You may argue that the need for trust is important for every relationship, but for the 6/2 Profile it is crucial.

The 6/2 Profile is also one of the four Left Angle Crosses. Unlike the Right Angle Crosses which have a Personal Destiny, the 6/2 has a Transpersonal Destiny. It is processing and understanding life through their interactions with others. Each person a 6/2 encounters is said to be karmic. Perhaps they made a prior agreement to meet in this lifetime. Each encounter is potentially transformational and life altering. Thus, interactions with people are not to be taken lightly for those with a Left Angle Cross.

Gifts

The gifts of the 6/2 Profile are many. Just imagine the innate genius of the 2nd Line connecting with the wisdom of the 6th Line, and you have a *shazam* potential. Look at some of the famous 6/2s: Isadora Duncan, George Lucas, Maya Angelou, Harry Truman, Mahatma Gandhi – powerful visionaries who have unleashed their potential.

The first gift, then, is that quality of genius or greatness that lies in wait to be seen and called out. The second gift is the capacity to demonstrate the possibility of living life in alignment with one's inner authority. 6/2 Profiles bring the needed cure for a world that has consistently looked outside themselves to an external authority. By turning within and living authentic lives, they usher in the new world. We could say that being true to themselves is their ultimate gift.

Challenges

The challenges of the 6/2 Profile begin with their triphasic journey. Those first thirty years of exploration, combined with not having a clear sense of their gifts, can be unstable as the 6th Line learns by bumping into life to see what doesn't work. With very little to stabilize them and a baseline insecurity, the experience can be rough. I spoke about my own challenges with this in Chapter 2.

The challenges continue into the second phase when the 6th Line is on the roof. While there is some relief in being out of the fire of trial-and-error exploration, there can be a feeling of not engaging in life at the level they sense they could or should be. During this phase they are figuring out just what is the impact they're here to make and how are they going to make it. The 2nd Line, during this phase, needs time alone and time to connect with their gifts and their genius. Again, this can be frustrating if they're watching other people thrive during these years. Think about it, with that Unconscious 2nd Line you have a person who knows they have something special to offer the world but can't exactly name it. With their Conscious 6th Line, you have a person with deep wisdom, but during that second phase the rubber isn't fully hitting the road.

In the third phase, the challenges have to do with integration and making the shift in identity to allowing oneself to be fully recognized – to claim and embody the Role Model. After years of not being recognized, it may seem like it's a big leap. But actually, it is a natural process. If they can stay true to their inner authority, they will find their way.

On another front, trust can be an issue for the 6/2 Profile. With an inherently positive spirit, if their trust is broken, it can be devastating. I know for myself, with my 6/2 Profile, that once someone has proven untrustworthy, I remain wary of them.

Other challenges the 6/2 face include their proclivity to distance. Unless they understand who they are, they can compare themselves with others who are comfortable being the center of attention. Judging themselves, they can abandon their natural style and develop defensive strategies to fit in. With their long-view vision, which sees things others may not yet see, they can also question their inner knowing when their vantage is not received. Finally, the 6/2 runs into trouble when it does not get the *hermit* time it needs to access its gifts.

WORKING WITH A 6/2 PROFILE

If your client has a 6/2 Profile, consider that they are wiser than they may show. Listen to what they see and know with curiosity. They may have something to say that you might not be able to appreciate. See if you can stretch beyond your limited perceptions. Support them to listen to their own inner authority, even if what they come up with seems out of the box.

Explain the three phases. Where are they on the triphasic trajectory? Perhaps they will benefit by doing some self-forgiveness work around those first thirty years. If they are in the second phase, they may feel frustrated that more things aren't happening for them. They can be late bloomers. Support them to be patient. They will get their time in the sun during the third phase. Help them to claim their Role Model self.

In relation to their 2nd Line, take time to notice their hidden gifts. They may look obvious to you but are not in your client's awareness. Can you name them or acknowledge them? Appreciate that the 2nd Line can feel a bit insecure. Can you help them open to their genius?

GUIDED MEDITATION

Imagine for a moment that you are a unique, once-in-a-lifetime being brought to Earth with a particular mission. You have an important purpose. What you have to bring is invaluable to the larger puzzle of humanity. Your light cannot be replicated by anyone else.

To ignite your purpose and ensure that your light is turned on, you've been given a gift: your Profile. You have been gifted the 6/2 Profile. This Profile gives you insight into how to realize your potential. It shows you the mechanism or the learning style that will call forth your purpose.

> *Take a moment to let go of the past and bring your focus to the present moment.*
> *Allow yourself to shift from ordinary consciousness to extraordinary consciousness.*
> *You are turning on the light of awareness to explore your 6/2 Profile.*
> *Begin by sensing your arms and legs.*
> *Let yourself arrive in your body.*
> *Breathe into your belly center.*
> *Gently stretch to find a comfortable resting place.*
> *Open to receive the power of your 6/2 Profile.*
> *You are here to be* the Role Model.
> *You have innate gifts that are waiting to be called out.*
> *Bring your awareness to your Conscious Line 6.*
> *Which phase of life are you in?*
> *Are you in your first thirty years of life where the 6th Line acts like the 3rd Line?*

If so, you are finding your way by trial and error.

Can you allow yourself to bump around?

Can you turn to your Strategy and Authority for guidance?

Or are you in the second phase of your Line 6 Profile – roughly age thirty to fifty?

Here your 6ᵗʰ line has gone on the roof, and you are learning through witnessing.

Notice how you feel some relief as you shift out of the first phase.

Perhaps you're in the last phase of life – from fifty onwards?

Have you integrated what you learned through trial and error and from witnessing?

Are you embodying your Role Model self?

Are you fully living your unique expression?

How does it feel?

Now, open to the Unconscious 2ⁿᵈ Line of your Profile.

Recognize yourself as someone who needs their hermit time.

You have gifts that you can't quite articulate.

They are seen when you take time to be in your own flow, doing what you love.

Now feel how the Line 6 and the Line 2 tend to hang back.

Can you relax and let others jump into the limelight, knowing your time will come?

Smile at your 6/2 Profile.

Ask it if there is any information your 6/2 Profile has for you.

Thank it.

And when you're ready, gently bring your awareness back to your body.

Sense your arms and legs.

Sense your belly center.

Take a breath.
And slowly bring your awareness back into the room.
Be still. Let what you have received integrate.
Take some time to anchor your experience by writing about
    it in your journal.

Note: If you want an audio recording of this meditation, reach out to
me with your Profile details at info@clientsandhumandesign.com.

16

THE 6/3 PROFILE

ROLE MODEL/MARTYR

Themes

- Triphasic

- Trial-and-error process can lead to wisdom

- Objectivity is key

- Bonds made and broken

- Resilient

- Honoring your own authority, you become a lighthouse for humanity

- Looking for soulmate

• Here to impact strangers of consequence

Entelechy: The 6/3 Profile is the last of the 12 Hexagrams. They are here to usher in a metamorphosis. By modeling what it means to live true to one's inner authority, they act as beacons. They show the way to a new world where each human being's uniqueness is honored.

Famous 6/3 Profiles

Steve Jobs, Serena Williams, JK Rowling, Leo Tolstoy, Joan Borysenko, Barbara Brennan (healer-Hands of Light), Marc Chagall, Matt Damon, Farrah Fawcett, Harrison Ford, Bill Murray, Colin Powell, Theodore Roosevelt, Dan Rather, Boris Johnson, Joan Rivers, Henri Rousseau, George Sand, Paulo Coelho

Overview

The 6/3 holds a special place in the context of the 12 pairs of Profiles. It is the last of the pairs and shines light on the transition that awaits humanity. There is a shift afoot, a fundamental change in our trajectory. Humans, in their quest for safety, have traditionally abdicated their authority. They have chosen to be led by others rather than listen within. The 6/3 Profile is here to show the new way. They are here to show that safety, in fact, lies in honoring our uniqueness and claiming our inner authority. The 6/3 Profile is the Role Model of living authentically, true to oneself.

The Conscious Line 6 and Unconscious Line 3 are in a harmonic. Both are oriented towards truth, though they take different paths in the discovery process. The Conscious 6th Line is looking at the big picture. It is concerned with integrity. It is focused on perfection in life. The Line 6 employs a witnessing approach, discerning from a detached awareness. As the wise souls they tap into their inner knowing and tune into their inner authority. Their heart's desire is to discover what's possible as they align with their authentic selves.

The Unconscious 3rd Line has a hands-on approach to truth. They throw themselves into the thick of life to determine what works and what doesn't work. Through this trial-and-error process, they gain wisdom. Their truth-finding results are garnered from an up close and personal embodied perspective.

Together, these two lines take the triphasic journey through life.

• For the first thirty years, they explore life as a double Line 3. (Remember, the 6th Line acts like a 3rd Line for those first thirty years.) During this phase, they are learning by experimentation and exploration. They are at times crashing into life to discover what does and doesn't work. It can be a bumpy ride for the 6/3 as they find their way in the material world. This discovery process includes relationships which can be precarious. The double Line 3 phase enters relationships and breaks off relationships in their search for what is right for them.

• From thirty to fifty, the Conscious 6th Line moves away from learning by exploration and shifts into a more distant witnessing approach. This creates some relief for the Unconscious 3rd line. While the Line 3 continues to learn by trial and error, it has the added support of perspective from the Conscious 6th Line vantage.

• After age fifty, if the wisdom of the first two phases integrates, the Role Model phase kicks in. The trial-and-error learnings are harvested along with the witnessing insights. The result is a rich maturity and wisdom as the 6/3 embodies their experience. With the Unconscious Line 3, the 6/3 never leaves the trial-and-error exploration, though it is done with more discernment. At this point, the 6/3 can begin to fulfill their role, fully living as the unique *being* that they are designed to be.

The cultivation of objectivity is key to the 6/3. Objectivity is the stabilizing force as the Unconscious Line 3 continues to draw the 6/3 out of their witness into the tumult of experimentation throughout the phases. With objectivity and an alignment with their unique authority comes ease and coherence in the midst of change.

While the 6th Line is looking for their soulmate, the 3rd Line has a bonds-made-and-broken approach. This can be a bit tricky in relationship. These lines both want the highest good, but the Conscious Line 6 can be threatened by the Unconscious Line 3.

Like the other 5th Lines, the 6/3 is here to impact strangers of consequence. Again, if we look at the list of famous people, we can see their unique and profound impact on people from a distance. In other words, their impact didn't take place in personal encounters.

THE CONSCIOUS LINE 6

The Role Model

The Conscious Line 6 is the witness. They are the old souls bearing wisdom. They see the big picture and comprehend things that aren't yet in other people's awareness. This can be frustrating and disheartening for the 6th line when their perceptions are not well received. Once they understand what they're up against, they can stop questioning themselves and judging others for the differences in perception.

As the witness, the 6th Line has a detached nature. They are standing back and watching life, especially after thirty. They tend to stand at the edge of a group watching rather than stepping into the inner circle.

THE UNCONSCIOUS LINE 3

The Martyr (The Experimenter)

The Unconscious Line 3 is dynamically alive living in the realm of wonder and curiosity. The world is their playground, and they want to taste and know all of it. What works? What doesn't work? They ask over and over with each thing they encounter. What's possible? Can this be improved? Their path is one of continuous experimentation and exploration. Once they have an answer, they share what they've learned with the world. This is the Unconscious aspect, so the trial and error may seem to happen to them rather than feeling like they are deliberately experimenting.

Nonetheless, the Unconscious 3rd Line is fully engaged with the material plane. Unafraid to challenge the status quo and anything in their path, they are looking to improve what's before them. Perpetual learners, they engage in life in a robust and wholehearted way. The 3rd Line's experimentation process is key to their wisdom development. Understanding this, they should never be criticized nor criticize themselves. Always, the question that supports the 3rd Line is, *What did you learn?*

Relationships for the 3rd Line are infused with a bonds-made-and-broken theme. When something is not working in a relationship, it's intolerable. They must shift it. This may look like pulling away to get more information about themselves or the person. It could be a permanent break, or the 3rd Line may come back with a new way of relating – a higher level of relationship coherence.

THE 6/3 PROFILE

The 6/3 Profiles are beacons, lighting the way to a new world order. Yet wherever there is change, there is uncertainty. Before the next highest order can evolve, there is a time of chaos. The

6/3 Profile has an inherently tumultuous path. They are aligning with an inner guidance system. This is not a smooth journey. The have an innate sense of perfection and are always approximating the next level of possibility. Meanwhile, they are living their uniqueness.

Consider for a moment 6/3 Steve Jobs. In his junior year of high school, he was described as "… an individual in a world where individuality was suspect." Throughout his career, Steve stayed true to his vision. He struggled to get others to understand his sensibility of what was possible with technology. He knew that computers would become personal appliances. He also understood they would one day be connected to each other. He was a perpetual inventor who was not afraid of failure, demanding his team create things that were seemingly impossible.

In relationship, while the 6th Line is looking for their soulmate, the 3rd Line has a bonds-made-and-broken approach. This can be a bit tricky. Staying with Steve Jobs as an example, he bounced around in relationships until, at age thirty-four, he met his soulmate sitting in the front row of a lecture he was giving at Stanford. Steve couldn't take his eyes off her. He met her in the parking lot after the lecture and asked her out to dinner, and they were inseparable until his death at fifty-six.

The 6/3 is the master of transformation. Resilient and capable of navigating the shifting world, they lead humanity in a new direction. The turn is away from the external as the authority to the internal guidance system. J.K. Rowling, another 6/3, wrote the wildly successful and highly impactful Harry Potter books. In them, she portrays Harry as the ultimate example of a 6/3. Again and again, in these stories, Harry bumps into life as he makes new discoveries. Relying on his own inner authority to navigate what seem like insurmountable challenges, he becomes a *role model* and a beacon of hope in the magical world. His life impacts the trajectory of the world.

The 6/3 Profile is the last of the four Left Angle Crosses. And while it is designed to follow its internal Authority, it does not, like the Right Angle Crosses, have a Personal Destiny. The 6/3 has a Transpersonal Destiny. They are processing and understanding their life through their interactions with others. Each meeting is said to be karmic. Each encounter is potentially life changing. Thus, interactions with people have a heightened importance for those with a Left Angle Cross.

Gifts

The gifts the 6/3 brings are noteworthy. They can have an unparalleled wisdom along with a profound objectivity. They are ushering in a new world of individuality. They herald a world where it is safe to be who you are. They are modeling a new way of living as your own authority, where what you need is sourced within. They also have the gift of a resilient nature and buoyant capacity to stay on their own trajectory.

My niece Lucy has a 6/3 Profile. As a kid, she had a great affinity for the *Baby-Sitters Club* books. This is a coming-of-age story about a diverse group of teenage girls. As a producer, Lucy helped bring the story to a successful Netflix series. Like Harry Potter, each of these girls is finding their way to living and being accepted as their unique selves. They are portraying the 6/3 Profile as they bumble through life, learning as they go, gathering wisdom along the way.

Challenges

One of the big challenges the 6/3 faces is navigating the tension between the two lines. As we said earlier, both Line 6 and Line 3 are in harmony with the purpose of knowing truth. However, they approach how they come to know that truth in dramatically different ways. Line 6 is focused on perfection and alignment. Line 3 is looking to see what is true by direct, in-the-moment experience. These can be at odds with each other or can work together.

Another major challenge the 6/3 must learn to navigate is the constant change the 3ʳᵈ Line brings. The 3ʳᵈ Line is continuously exploring. It's on a mission to unearth what works and what doesn't work. In relationship, this looks like connecting then disconnecting with people. The 6ᵗʰ Line likes more stability. They are not comfortable with the 3ʳᵈ Line M.O. The 6/3 needs to navigate this internal difference. It's helpful if they have people in their lives who they trust will stay connected while they go through this process. It may look like the 3ʳᵈ Line is not committed in relationship when actually they are looking for higher levels of coherence.

With the constant change the 3ʳᵈ Line brings, there can be incredible chaos and destabilization in the 6/3's life. They are not following the rules set out by others. Instead, they are making their own way. They are challenging the status quo. In 2018, Serena Williams disrupted the tennis world with her choice of clothing. She wore a full-body catsuit at the French Open. But this wasn't the first time she'd been attacked for showing up in alignment with herself. In this case, she said she wore the catsuit for her health (she was battling blood clots postpartum) and to inspire mothers. Serena has dealt with a lifetime of microaggressions, starting as a teenager being mocked for her beaded hair. Another Profile might not have had the resiliency to take the risks that Serena did.

Think about what it takes to step out and show up in a world where we are conditioned to believe we are safe when we blend. This is the edge the 6/3 navigates. In the early 1900s, Marc Chagall was a Jewish artist in Imperial Russia. It was a time of *pogroms* and serious education and travel restrictions for Jews. To be an artist at that time, he had two choices: he could deny his Jewish roots, or he could embrace them. As an assertion of his self, he incorporated his Jewish identity into all of his works.

With their passion for perfection, the 6/3 can be challenging for other people. Steve Jobs was described as a demanding perfectionist. Serena Williams got very upset with tennis officials who made inaccurate line calls.

WORKING WITH A 6/3 PROFILE

When you are working with a 6/3 Profile, think about their life as a journey. Where are they on that triphasic path?

It's crucial for 6/3 children to be supported during the first trial-and-error phase. If they were shamed for their trial-and-error learning style, it can impact their whole lives. They need to experience knowing that they can try things, have them not work out, and use what they learned to go forward. If your client did not get that support, there will be work to do deconditioning the belief that mistakes are detrimental.

Remember that you may encounter upheaval or disorder as the 6/3 creates chaos before a new level of coherence is established. Can you tolerate it? Can you support your client to call on their witnessing capacity to bring a modicum of ground while they bump around? Can you call on the observing 6th Line to bring objectivity?

Can you trust your 6/3 client to tap into their inner authority rather than support them to look for outer safety? Can you celebrate their "failures" as learning opportunities? Can you recognize and acknowledge their resilience? My niece Lucy texted me this morning. She's gotten a few "insane" job offers. She tells me she hopes she's making the right choice. I remind her that as a 6/3, she can't know ahead of time. She has to try it out to see. She texts back, "It's so hard!" I remind her that she has the resiliency to do it.

When it comes to relationships, help 6/3s understand that

they do well with a partner who can tolerate their need to attach then separate. Remind them that their 3rd Line will always need time on its own to interact with life separate from others.

GUIDED MEDITATION

Imagine for a moment that you are a unique, once-in-a-lifetime being brought to Earth with a particular mission. You have an important purpose. You are bringing an invaluable piece to the larger puzzle of humanity. Your light cannot be replicated by anyone else.

To ignite your purpose and ensure that your light is turned on, you've been given a gift: your Profile. You have been gifted the 6/3 Profile. This Profile gives you insight into how to realize your potential. It shows you the mechanism or the learning style that will call forth your purpose.

> Take a moment to let go of the past and shift your focus to
> the present moment.
> Allow yourself to shift from ordinary consciousness to
> extraordinary consciousness.
> You are turning on the light of awareness to explore your
> 6/3 Profile.
> Begin by sensing your arms and legs.
> Let yourself arrive in your body.
> Take breath into your belly center.
> Gently stretch to find a comfortable resting place.
> Recognize that you have an important role to play in
> humanity's evolution.
> You are here to model what it means to live as your
> authentic self.
> You are here to show that it is safe to be unique.
> You are here to help people see it's possible to live
> according to their own inner authority.

You have a journey of maturity that sometimes looks quite bumpy.

Take some time now to look more closely at your 6/3 Profile.

Bring your awareness to your Conscious 6th Line.

Which phase of life are you in?

Are you in your first thirty years of life, where the 6th Line acts like the 3rd Line?

If so, you are relying heavily on experimentation to find your way.

Can you allow yourself to bump around?

Can you turn to your Strategy and Authority for guidance?

Or are you in the second phase of your 6th Line Profile – roughly age thirty to fifty?

Here, your Line 6 has gone on the roof, and you are including learning through witnessing.

Notice how your 3rd Line gets some ground with this new perspective.

Notice, too, that your 3rd Line continues to pull you into learning by engaging with life.

Perhaps you're in the last phase of life – from fifty onwards?

Here you have integrated what you learned through trial and error and from witnessing?

Are you embodying your Role Model self?

Are you fully living your unique expression?

How does it feel?

Now, open to the Unconscious 3rd Line of your Profile.

Recognize yourself as someone who is here to learn by thoroughly engaging in life.

You need to try things out to see what doesn't work so you can get clear on what does.

You are gathering much-needed information.

There are no mistakes here.

*Only information you learn that brings you closer to
     truth.*

*Take a moment to recognize the 3rd and 6th Lines in action
     together.*

Feel how the Conscious 6th Line has long vision.

*The Unconscious 3rd Line has the up close and personal
     information.*

Feel the 6th Line's tendency to hang back.

The 3rd Line's tendency to want to jump in.

How are you navigating that difference?

Smile at your 6/3 Profile.

Ask it if there is any information your Profile has for you.

Thank it.

*And when you're ready, gently bring your awareness back
     to your body.*

Sense your arms and legs.

Sense your belly center.

Take a breath.

And slowly bring your awareness back into the room.

Be still. Let what you have received integrate.

*Take some time to anchor your experience by writing about
     it in your journal.*

Note: If you want an audio recording of this meditation, reach out to
me with your Profile details at info@clientsandhumandesign.com.

USING THE PROFILES WITH YOUR CLIENTS

Now that you've got a handle on the 12 Profiles, it's time to take this knowledge to your clients, your family, your colleagues, and your friends. It's time to work with the information in real time. This can be done in a light, playful way or in a deep, exploratory way. You can share the information you get, or you can keep it to yourself for your own knowledge. You'll know what to do in each situation. But first, you'll need to have their charts. You can download charts for free here: https://clientsandhumandesign. com/free-chart/.

Now that you've got their chart, the next step is to read the chapter on their Profile. Sit with it. Receive it. Be curious about what it means for them in their lives. Does it fit from your vantage? Be wary of the ego's desire to put people in boxes. It's easy to use any system – this one included – to pigeonhole people. We do that when we want to know something, when we want to feel secure, or when we want to have control. This is the antithesis of Human Design. We're using the Profiles as an exploration – a starting place and a doorway into understanding. Keep your curiosity engaged! Use the Profiles to open doors of possibility, not to confine people into labels.

It's a funny thing about the Profiles. They give you all this immediate information that's super helpful. They can stand alone, meaning you don't have to understand any other parts of the Human Design system and still use the Profiles to great advantage. And yet they are one part of a bigger system. The more aspects of Human Design you understand, the more powerful your capacity to meet your client in their exploration of themselves.

Let's say for example your client is a 1/3 Projector. That might look very different from a 1/3 Manifesting Generator. In each of these cases, the way the person goes about investigating might vary dramatically. The explorations might look very different. A 1/3 Projector might need to wait for an invitation to explore something. The 1/3 Manifesting Generator might be all over the place exploring. In my first book on Types, I likened the Projectors to cats and the Generators and Manifesting Generators to working dogs. Consider how differently a dog gathers information and explores their world compared to a cat. There are similarities, yes, but how they interface with the environment is different. The 1/3 Projector might have less energy for exploration than the Manifesting Generator. If we go to the next level of refinement, the Projector with a Defined Will Center likely has a more robust and engaged-in-life exploration than a Projector with an Open Will Center. The Will Center is engaged with the material world.

Think again of someone with many Defined Centers as opposed to someone with a large number of Open Centers. The person with substantial definition in their chart may be more grounded in their exploration. The person with a lot of openness may be more influenced by the people around them in terms of what they choose to investigate and explore. Their exploration might look more fluid, less grounded.

If someone has strong Tribal Circuitry they may be inclined to investigate and explore within the tribal context. Their energies may be exploring passion, lovemaking, agreements, sustainability, food, or business. With a preponderance of Individual Circuitry, they may be called to investigate unusual or unique things and explore areas others wouldn't think to traverse. With a focus on Collective Circuitry, they may be exploring how to share what they've discovered, or what laws or structures to create to benefit humanity. If they have a dynamic tension between their Individual and Tribal Circuitry, they may be exploring showing up authentically versus blending in.

We can home in even further by looking at the Gates and their placement in the chart.

If someone has a 1/3 Profile and their Sun is in Gate 47, The Mindset Gate, they may focus their investigation and exploration on mindset. Who has what mindset? What happens when they have a positive mindset? What happens when they have a negative mindset? If Mercury, the planet of communication is in Gate 47, the 1/3 Profile might be investigating how to articulate issues around mindset.

You can begin to see the nuances as we weave together the pieces of the chart. We can also look at Profiles in relation to others. Say, for example, if one person in a couple has a 1/3 Profile and another person has a 2/4 Profile, they are going to have very different needs and styles. The 1/3 will be more self-focused, and while the 2/4 has a *hermit* side, they will be called to be in social situations in networks with people. If you know your partner has a 4/1 Profile, you will give them more space than you might otherwise give someone. You will know that they are not designed to be flexible and that you will have to be the one to shift in relation to them.

THE PROFILES IN RELATIONSHIP TO OTHERS

When you put two charts together, it's called a connection chart. Another way to work with differences in a relationship is to see which Centers (if any) remain open when you put the charts together. Those Open Centers are the place the couple is going to be exploring. For example, if a 2/4 and a 3/6 share an Open Will Center, they will be exploring what they value. How they go about it will be different. The 3/6 will jump in with experimentation. The 2/4 may be journaling, painting, or taking walks to discover what they value. On the other hand, they may be connecting with people in their network to gather information about different possible values.

We have talked about different lines being in harmony within the Profiles: Line 1 is in harmony with Line 4, Line 2 is in harmony with Line 5, and Line 3 is in harmony with Line 6. The Profiles that have two numbers in harmony are rarer: the 1/4, 2/5, 3/6, 4/1, 5/2, and 6/3. We can also look at harmony and resonance between the Profile numbers. I have a 6/2 Profile. My 6 is in resonance with people who have 6th Lines and in harmony with people who have 3rd Lines. My Line 2 is in resonance with other 2nd Lines and in harmony with people who have 5th Lines. So, we could say I am resonating and harmonizing with Lines 2, 3, 5, and 6 – in other words, anyone with a 2/5, 3/6, 5/2, 6/2, or 6/3 Profile. Line 1 and 4 are out of my resonance frequency. They are more different than similar. How might this information play out?

My wife and I both have 6/2 Profiles. There is a kind of simpatico in the way we approach life. We like our *hermit* time. We tend to stay on the outskirts of groups. There's a familiarity in our approach to life. We share a deep wisdom. We value each other's insights. Meanwhile, we have friends and family with 2/4 Profiles whose social stamina is baffling to us.

Take my sister Heidi, for example. She has a 2/4 Profile. She and I resonate with the shared 2nd Line. We are looking at and admiring each other's hidden gifts. We are calling one another out. Where we differ, we are in awe of each other. She recognizes my 6th Line wisdom, and I am blown away by her 4th Line capacity to create networks.

Let's look at another example. I have a client who is a 2/4 and has kids who have 1/3 Profiles. She connects with her children where they have a harmonic: the Line 1 and Line 4 harmonic. They connect through investigation. That is their common ground. The kids see and respect their mom's need for *hermit* time, though that is not their style. The mom understands the kids' need to learn by trial and error, but that is not exactly comfortable for her.

Can you see how you might look at relationships and find the resonance or harmonic as a place to connect? Can you see how you might look at the places that don't have resonance or a harmonic as places to learn from the other?

Let me give another example. My coach, Angela Lauria, is a 3/5. When we are together, her Line 3 and my Line 6 are in harmonic. She can nudge me to get messy with life and try on things that are uncomfortable. *Why not?* Her Line 3 asks. My Line 6 can invite her to step back and witness the world from a bigger vantage. After all, we both want truth. We can support one another in that endeavor. My 2nd Line is also in harmony with her 5th Line. We're both a bit shy. We both get projected on. I admire her zest and practical solutions as a savior of humanity. Perhaps she sees my hidden talents?

What happens when there is no resonance? Say my 6/2 Profile in relation to a 1/4 or 4/1 Profile. What then? You might think, *Well, that's not going to be a good match.* Don't go there! I happen to love and appreciate difference. Some of my closest friends have a 1/4 or 4/1 Profile. I find them fascinating.

What is your Profile, your partner's, or your Client's? How do you interface?

For those who like to get down and dirty,

• The 1/3 Profile resonates with and is in harmony with Lines 1, 3, 4, and 6 – so, Profiles 1/3, 1/4, 2/4, 3/5, 3/6, 4/1, 4/6, 5/1, 6/2, and 6/3. They are different from the 2/5 and 5/2 Profiles.

• The 1/4 Profile resonates with and is in harmony with Lines 1 and 4, which means they connect with 1/3, 1/4, 2/4, 4/6, 4/1, and 5/1 Profiles. They are different from 2/5, 3/5, 3/6 5/2, 6/2, and 6/3 Profiles.

• The 2/4 Profile resonates with and is in harmony with Lines 1, 2, 4, and 5. So, they connect with the 1/4, 2/4, 2/5, 3/5, 4/6, 4/1, 5/1, 5/2, and 6/2 Profiles. They are different from the 3/6, and 6/3 Profiles.

• The 2/5 Profile resonates with and is in harmony with Lines 2 and 5. So, they are connected with the 2/4, 2/5, 3/5, 5/1, 5/2, and 6/2 Profiles. They are different from the 1/3, 1/4, 3/6, 4/6, and 4/1 Profile.

• The 3/5 Profile resonates with and is in harmony with Lines 2, 3, 5, and 6. They are connected with the 1/3, 2/5, 3/5, 3/6, 4/6, 5/1, 5/2, 5/3, and 6/2 Profiles. They are different from the 1/4 and 4/1 Profiles.

• The 3/6 Profile resonates with and is in harmony with Lines 3 and 6. Therefore, they connect with the 1/3, 3/5, 3/6, 4/6, 6/2, and 6/3 Profiles. They are different from the 1/4, 2/4, 2/5, 4/1, 5/1, and 5/2 Profiles.

• The 4/6 Profile resonates and is in harmony with Lines 1, 3, 4, and 6. They connect with the 1/3, 1/4, 2/4, 3/5, 3/6, 4/6, 4/1,

5/1, 5/3, 6/2, and 6/3. They are different from the 2/5 and 5/2 Profiles.

• The 4/1 Profile resonates with and is in harmony with Lines 1 and 4. Therefore, they connect with the 1/3, 1/4, 2/4, 4/6, 4/1, and 5/1 Profiles. They are different from 2/5, 3/5, 3/6, 5/2, 6/2, and 6/3 Profiles.

• The 5/1 Profile resonates with and is in harmony with the Lines 1, 2, 4, and 5. They connect with the 1/3, 1/4, 2/4, 2/5, 3/5, 4/6, 4/1, 5/1, 5/2, and 6/2 Profiles. They are different from the 3/6 and 6/3 Profiles.

• The 5/2 Profile resonates with and is in harmony with the Lines 2 and 5. So, they are connected with the 2/4, 2/5, 3/5, 5/1, 5/2, and 6/2 Profiles. They are different from the 1/3, 1/4, 3/6, 4/6, and 4/1 Profiles.

• The 6/2 Profile resonates with and is in harmony with the Lines 2, 3, 5, and 6. They connect with the 1/3, 2/4, 2/5, 3/5, 3/6, and 4/6 Profiles. They are different from the 1/4 and 4/1 Profiles.

• The 6/3 Profile resonates with and is in harmony with the Lines 3 and 6. Therefore, they connect with the 1/3, 3/5, 3/6, 4/6, 6/2, and 6/3 Profiles. They are different from the 1/4, 2/4, 2/5, 4/1, 5/1, and 5/2 Profiles.

Can you see that the exploration of differences in Profiles could be rich and informative for your clients? If you have a context for what you're doing in relation to your Profile and you and your partner or client understand your Profiles, you can organize at a different level of coherence together.

Working with Your Clients

The first thing you have to be clear on when working with your clients and their Profiles is to understand your own Profile. What is your inclination? Are you someone who takes a trial-and-error approach? Are you an information gatherer? Are you naturally friendly? Are you prone to work with people you know or perhaps with people you don't know?

• If you have a 1st Line Profile, you are going to use information gathering as a tool.

• If you have a 2nd Line Profile, you have a *hermit* side and hidden gifts that you may or may not recognize.

• If you have a 3rd Line Profile, you are going to favor a trial-and-error learning style.

• If you have a 4th Line Profile, working with people you know and who come through your network is key to your success. You'll have a friendly, personal style.

• If you have a 5th Line Profile, you will do best working with strangers. You'll be waiting for the right call to step in and bring solutions.

• If you have a 6th Line Profile, you will be looking at the long view and bringing wisdom to the table. You also will do best working with strangers.

Once you're clear on what you're bringing and how you best work, it's time to be clear on your client's path. What will best support them? What is *their* style?

I've been in many coaching groups, and I'm keenly aware of

how coaches assume that their style is *the way*. I've seen coaches with 3rd Line Profiles teach trial and error as the path. I've seen coaches with 5th Lines assume that people are here to solve a problem. I've seen 4th Line coaches teach a style of friendliness and connection as a marketing tool. Each one of their approaches is brilliant and useful. They just may not be a match for the person you're working with. It'd be like telling a Projector they should act like a Generator.

Can we learn from these different styles? Yes. Can we try them on? Yes. But our success is going to come when we're aligned with our own Profile and when we are following our unique Strategy and Authority.

That said, if you have a client with a Line 1 Profile, you are going to want to support them to take all the time they need gathering information. This will give them a foundation and confidence – a place to move from. You are likewise going to want to give them as much detailed information as you have. I mentioned that when I give a Human Design coaching session to someone with a 1st Line Profile, I go out of my way to cover all the details of the chart. I know this brings a ground and ease to that Line 1. Don't underestimate this need and how gratifying information can be for them.

If you have a client with a Line 2 in their Profile, you will want to be curious about their hidden gifts. Reflect them as you see them. Call them out. Also, support your client to have unimpeded time doing what they love. Trust that in that space, they are magnetic and pull the people and situations to them that will call forth their gifts.

Just a side note story about my own experience with this Unconscious Line 2. In 1997, I attended The School for The Work with Byron Katie. It was the first time she offered it, and about thirteen of us were in Barstow with Katie for three weeks doing *The Work* day and night. I assisted at her second school, pared down to two weeks. During that time, I got a nasty gum infection. Averse to Western medicine, I refused antibiotics and instead tried a slew of alternatives. I was not well. I continued to show up to the sessions, but my "nice" persona was nowhere in sight. Eventually, I took the antibiotics. Of course, I had an allergic reaction to them and ended up covered in welts. By this time, all of my relational strategies were out the window. I was in my *hermit* self in the midst of the program. Self-focused, I had no capacity to caretake others. From my perspective, I was a horrible assistant. I was convinced I would never be invited back to be on support staff. I was shocked when Katie asked me to be her righthand person for the schools. I had no clue what she saw in me. Over the next two years in that position, I discovered the gifts she recognized and valued from the beginning.

If you have a client with a Line 3 Profile, you want to encourage their trial-and-error learning process. Have them look back at their life and see what they have learned when things didn't work out. Have them do an inventory. Are they blaming themselves for "mistakes?" Can you help them to reframe those situations? Can you support them to find a new narrative that gives them full permission, in alignment with their Strategy and Authority, to explore life in a hands-on way? Can you help them see how vital it is to their success to learn what does work by finding out what doesn't? Remember that if someone has a 6th Line in their Profile, they will act like a 3rd Line during their first thirty years.

If you have a client with a Line 4 in their Profile, you will want to have the discussion regarding network. Do they have a good network? If not, that is the first thing that needs to be addressed and rectified. Emphasize the importance of their network. Utilize their network in marketing. Call on their friendliness to connect with people as a path to success. Help them understand the vulnerability of the 4th Line and the need for stability. Know how important their network is to them and help them to feel it. I've had clients who, once they understood their gift of networking (and that they weren't designed to market to everyone), experience newfound success. It's striking what difference understanding oneself from a new vantage can make.

Another side story. I spoke earlier about my 3/5 book and business coach Angela Lauria. She has that Profile that is going to save the world by seeing what doesn't work and making corrections. She midwifed hundreds of people to write books and make a difference. This past year, she became friends with Marianne Williamson and invited Marianne to be part of The Author Incubator. Marianne is a 2/4. Remember, with a Line 5, Angela is designed to solve the problem and step out. She is not the person to be focused on creating community. That is not her long suit. When Marianne showed up, things shifted. We met every Wednesday with Marianne for "Author Church." Marianne began creating community. She wanted to know who we were. She wanted connection. She wanted intimacy. Her long suit wasn't so much as a problem solver. Her long suit was connection. She created conversations that had an impact. She brought her 2nd Line genius to people in her individual conversations with them. Being part of her network shifted how we thought. It changed how we approached our writing. She called on us to think more broadly and to include the political world in our dialogue. Marianne called us to network.

If you have a client with a Line 5 in their Profile, understand that they have a big job. They are truly here to save the world. This can be felt as a burden or as an exhilarating possibility or both. The conversation around projection looms large and will need to be untangled. How can they live skillfully in the projection field? Can they use the projections rather than take them personally? Another conversation you'll want to explore is around the call. What is a good call? Are they following their Strategy and Authority to discern a good call and then using the awareness of when it is time to step out? Is the job over? Can they hand it off to others to complete? They must have time to recuperate between callings. All these are key to their wellbeing and effectiveness.

Finally, if you have a client with a Line 6 in their Profile, remember to address the triphasic path. Where are they on that journey? What were their first thirty years like? What was/is their time on the roof like? If they are on the roof, they may be frustrated that they are not out in the world enough. Have they come to their Kiron Return? Know that their time will come. Support them to be patient. Look for the wisdom of your 6th Line client. Listen to what they have to say. Encourage them to follow their inner authority.

For each of the different Profiles, you will want to adjust the lens you look through and open to see how they see and experience the world. Seeing and reflecting them through their Profile could be the biggest gift you give them.

18

CHALLENGES ON THE PATH

OK, so, you've delved into the Profiles. You're using them with your clients. It's amazing. You're turned on. You want to know and work with everyone's Profile. Then again, maybe you're starting to run into some roadblocks...

You don't have someone's birth information, especially an accurate birth time. How do you work with their profile?

Someone doesn't resonate with their Profile. How do you respond?

You're excited to use this new technology but are met with suspicion.

You're frustrated when you don't know someone's Profile.

Suddenly, you're seeing the complexities of integrating the Profiles into the whole chart.

Let's take a look at these challenges.

Birth Chart Issues

This is a very real challenge. If you want an accurate Human Design chart, you must have the accurate birth time, place, and date. Fortunately, if you are simply wanting to find a person's

Profile, it can be worked with relatively easily. If you live in the United States and you want the accurate chart, you can have your client check the county records office. If it's not on the birth certificate, it can often be found there.

But let's say you want the Profile information, and you don't have access to the birth time. You can do the trial-and-error process of running charts throughout the day and looking to see when or if the Profile changes. Start at 00:01 then run the chart every two hours. The next chart you run would be 2:00 a.m., then 4:00 a.m., et cetera. Most likely, you won't have more than one or two Profile changes throughout the day, which leaves with you two or three Profiles – maybe four in an unusual case. You can then take those Profiles and ask a series of questions to help you determine which Profile. For example, if they have a 1st Line in the Profile, you can ask if they are drawn to gathering information and if they need information to feel safe. If they have a 4th Line, you can ask about being social or about being someone with a network. When I ran my friend Sara's chart, it said she had a 2/4 Profile. For a year, I talked to her about her network. I tried to nudge her in the direction of networking. It just didn't pan out for her. Then, we discovered we had the time wrong. She was actually a 3/5. That made so much more sense. We both felt the truth of it. Consider how it feels to them. If one of the possible times has a 5th Line, ask them if they feel like they're here to save the world. Do they get projected on?

Play around. Have them help you. Oftentimes, when people don't have an exact birth time, they may just have an idea of what time of day they were born, like in the morning or in the evening. That helps narrow down the choices too.

If you're unable to figure it out, you can always refer them to a Human Design practitioner who will be able to ask more complex questions, taking in the whole of the chart. Or you could refer them to an astrologer who does birth chart rectifica-

tions. I find Vedic astrology particularly good with time recti-
fication.

So, you run the chart, get the Profile, and the person doesn't
resonate. There are a couple of possibilities here. One possibility, like with my friend Sara, is that you've got the wrong time.
Did you confuse a.m. and p.m.? I've definitely done that! Or
maybe the time was entered wrong on the birth certificate. You
can always run the chart fifteen minutes to a half hour on either
side to see if the Profile changes. If you're pretty sure you've got
the right time and the right Profile, and the person doesn't
resonate, then consider a) there is a mitigating factor in their
chart that has to be taken into account, or b) they are not in
alignment with themselves.

Usually, people will resonate with their Profile. They will
recognize themselves. They will feel seen. Often, there is a
relief. Occasionally, they will be stumped by some aspect of it.
Take my client, who is a 1/3 Manifestor. She is one of those
Manifestors who was stuffed in a box and not allowed to have
her voice. She is in the process of reclaiming her Manifestor
power. Meanwhile, while she definitely resonates with the 1st
Line Investigator, she doesn't see herself as an explorer. Trial
and error petrifies her.

There are a few things we can see here. One, as a child, the
Unconscious 3rd Line took the hit, along with her Manifestor
aspect. It wasn't safe to show up, have a voice, or experiment.
What she does remember is that she liked to experiment with
moving her furniture around in her bedroom. That was doable.
The second thing to take into account is that the 3rd Line is
actually unconscious. It takes awareness to recognize it. We
don't necessarily go around identifying with our Unconscious
Profile.

Working with her, I recognized her 1/3 Profile. She definitely
was more personal than transpersonal. She is in her own world
figuring out answers by doing research. Our work focused on

finding out what information she needed before she could step out and do her exploring.

Suspicion

The next challenge you may meet as you approach people to work with their Profile is suspicion. It's true, getting someone's birth information can be a bit tricky. I recently did a training for business entrepreneurs and asked for the participants' birth info so I could have their charts for the training. One person didn't feel comfortable sharing her birth info. This happens. Another person didn't want me to know her age. In these cases, I suggest you give them the link to run their own charts and ask them to give you their Profile.

The bigger suspicion regarding using the birth time is another matter. People who question astrology can be put off when they realize Human Design has an astrological element. This can be especially true in the business world. My brother David, who graduated from Harvard with his MBA and spent his life as a major CEO of large companies, was one such person. He reluctantly agreed to have me run his and his family's chart at a family reunion years ago. Without abandoning his air of being on the high side of knowing, he looked at me and said, "Robin, I have to admit, this is uncannily accurate."

Times are changing. Human Design is spreading like wildfire. More and more people are familiar with it. In a matter of time, it will be as mainstream as yoga has become, which is to say, if someone is not comfortable with it and not willing to see if it has any relevance for them, let it go. There came a time in my psychotherapy practice when I stopped taking clients who wouldn't let me run their charts. It just didn't make sense to me not to have the wealth of information that would fast track our work.

Frustration

Next, let's take a brief look at the frustration that is bound to arise when you don't know someone's Profile. I feel this when I'm on group coaching calls and someone is processing with a coach. I know I could help them with their book project and with their marketing if only I knew their Profile (and the rest of their chart!). I know I could help the coach work with them more skillfully. Often, I will send a private message offering to run their chart. More often than not, they take me up on it. I find it's a kindness to share people's charts with them.

The Elephant in the Room

You've got the gist of the Profiles. You see they are a simple and immediate way to understand and work with people. You also are starting to realize that there is so much more. There is a world of nuance and complexity when you look at the Profiles within the context of the different aspects of the chart. Those will take time to master.

Maybe your client is a 1/3 Projector with their Conscious Sun in Gate 37, which emanates the quality of Friendship. Friendships are big in this chart, but the 1/3 Profile is more about themselves. How does your client navigate those differences?

Maybe your client is a 2/5 Manifesting Generator. They are needing to navigate the pull to hide out with the push to speak, be heard, and impact. This can be quite confusing. It takes time to integrate what you have learned. It takes time to explore and gather information about the Profiles through experience. There is no end to the exploration.

HOW FLUENT DO YOU WANT TO BE IN HUMAN DESIGN?

Human Design is like learning a language. Say you want to visit to France. You learn the French words you need to navigate your trip. *Where is the bathroom? Where is the train station?* But if you decide to live in France and want to read the newspaper in French or read a poem written in French, it's going to take some more study on your part. It's not a big deal if you take it piece by piece. Of course, it's helpful to be in a context where you can practice with people and speak the language.

Obviously, I'm a proponent of learning the Human Design language. I write these books to share the knowledge. I'm committed to making the information easily accessible. I teach people how to be conversant in Human Design. I train coaches to incorporate Human Design in their work. That's my dharma.

Are you called to learn more?

19

UNLEASHING POTENTIAL

We've come to the end of this leg of our journey together. This is the moment where we pause, reflect on our experience, and then consider our next steps.

You've learned the fundamentals of the Human Design Profile. You know what the Profile is. You understand the 6 Lines of the Hexagram. You've been introduced to the 12 Profiles. Hopefully, you've run charts of your clients, your family, and your friends, and you are actively working with the Profiles.

Take a moment and contemplate what you discovered. What are your key takeaways? Is your life different now that you have this information? Do you work with clients differently? If so, how?

I'm trusting that your left brain has been nourished with pragmatic information. You have a new foundation to stand on and work with.

I'm hoping that learning more about yourself and others has touched you, moved you, and opened you to new possibilities.

Maybe you've had an experience of connecting directly with the energy of the 6 Lines and the 12 Profiles. Do they speak to you? Can you feel them? Have they become a transformational force in your life?

Can you see how naturally and easily you can use the Profiles with great benefit?

Perhaps on this journey, you've stepped into a transformational healing vortex. In recognizing different learning styles, you've made more space for people to be who they are. You're more respectful and curious rather than judgmental and dismissive. You know better than to think your way is superior. You've entered the next level of your journey. You are putting the left-brain information into action.

Can you imagine from your new vantage how different the world might be if parents knew their children's Profiles? Can you imagine how impactful coaches and therapists might be if they knew their clients' Profiles? Can you image how employers might benefit from knowing their employee's Profiles? How differently might we relate to one another if we knew our family's, friends', and lover's Profiles? Can you imagine if we respected and honored people's Profiles?

We are raised to be homogenized, to blend, and to fit in. That survival strategy has worked well for centuries. With the turning tides, it is no longer viable. These times call for coherence through complexity and diversity.

Following a brain injury, I studied the Anat Baniel Method to bring my brain back online. I discovered from Anat that as children, we learn to walk in a way that works for us. It may not be optimal, but it's good enough for our little bodies. As we age and mature, and as we put on weight, we require more from our bodies. What we learned as children is no longer optimal. We start having hip pain or back pain or knee pain. Our alignment does not support our activity. Walking, for instance, requires a high level of differentiation. We begin to struggle when the level of differentiation no longer matches what's needed as we navigate the dynamic tension between stability and mobility.

If we don't know better, as we age, we stop differentiating. Our culture assumes this is an inevitable part of aging. It is not. When an elder person falls, it's most likely due to the lack of differentiation in their feet and ankles. They cannot feel the object beneath them. The muscles and bones in their feet and ankles don't register the difference and respond accordingly. They fall.

When we do not know our Profile, we're in an undifferentiated state of awareness. We act without that poise between mobility and stability. We fall, not understanding why.

The more complexity and diversity we can embrace within ourselves and within humanity, the more highly functional we become.

Becoming proficient with the Profiles, and the other aspects of Human Design, increases our differentiation. With this, we have the capacity to stand in who we are and bring what we're here to bring into action. And we have the skill to support others to do the same. All of humanity benefits.

I come from a rafting family. Growing up, we'd sit around the campfire at night, playing games after a long day on the river. One game was called Crossed/Uncrossed. One of my brothers would take two sticks, talk about something, or make a gesture, then pass the sticks to the person next to him saying either, *I'm passing these crossed,* or *I'm passing these uncrossed.* Sometimes, he would cross his arms as he passed the sticks; sometimes, he wouldn't. It didn't seem to have any bearing on what he said. If the sticks had been passed crossed, the next person then would say *I'm taking these crossed (or uncrossed) and passing them uncrossed (or crossed).* If you knew the trick of the game, you knew immediately if they got it right. You'd know what they did to determine if the sticks were passed crossed or uncrossed. If you got it wrong, you were out of the game.

I could never figure this game out. I always got it wrong. I listened to everything people said as they passed the sticks. I watched everything they did. It made no sense to me. Until one night, I saw. It had nothing to do with what people said or what they did with their arms. That was all distraction. It was so simple really.

It took awareness. It took discernment. It took differentiation.

You see, I was correct in seeing that it had nothing to do with what the person did with their arms or what they said. What mattered was what they did with their legs. If their legs were crossed, then they were passing (or receiving) the sticks crossed. If their legs were uncrossed, they were passing (or receiving) the sticks uncrossed.

Once it was clear, it was obvious. Just like the Profiles. It doesn't matter what you're doing out in the world if you don't know what's going on below the surface. If you try to market like a 4th Line when you've got a 2/5 Profile, you're going to flounder. If you know your Profile, you stay in the game. And right now, we need everyone in the game.

You're someone who can help people stay in the game. You can see and support people to recognize who they are, differentiate, and bring the gifts they were meant to bring to the world.

You can help people live their dharma.

When you do, you call forth people's unique genius.

You unleash their potential.

You are part of solution that ushers in the next level of coherence following the chaos.

ILLUSTRATIONS

Charts

#1 Finding the Profile

#2 Marianne Williamson: 2/4 Profile

#3 Angela Lauria: 3/5 Profile

#4 The 6 Lines of the Hexagram

#5 The 6 Lines of the Hexagram with Names

#6 The 6 Lines with Names

#7 The 12 Profiles by Crosses

#8 The 12 Profiles

ACKNOWLEDGMENTS

As I complete this, my third book in as many years, I'm in awe of the process. There is dance between structure and flow that enables the conception and birth of a book.

I am profoundly grateful for the connection to Source that allows me to surrender to the flow. I have Open Head, Open Ajna, Open Throat, Open G, and Open Will Centers. I don't know what I'm going to say until I say it. Only in partnership with Spirit can *The Voice* speak through me. The words in this book don't belong to me. They come through me in service to you. My apologies for any place where my ego's voice has slipped in. That was not my intent.

The Author Incubator process provides a structure, a ground for the flow. It gives me a step-by-step template to follow in a specific time frame. There are no outs. The deadlines are firm. My sneaky self has no room to negotiate or wiggle. The book will be done by this time, and these are the things I have to do to get there. Period. End of story. One brick at time creates a wall. Discipline. Structure. (OK, so I've been reading the story of Will Smith in *Will* by Mark Manson – thus, the brick/wall analogy. Read the book!)

Thank you, Angela Lauria for creating The Author Incubator to support authors to have a voice and ensure they get their books written! Your invitation to step in and become the person who writes the book and makes a difference has dramatically shifted the trajectory of my life. Seriously empowering. I am forever grateful.

This past year, Angela invited Marianne Williamson to be part of the program. Each week, a small group of us met with Marianne in "Author Church." Here we discussed what it meant to be an author and the responsibility that entails. We looked at current world events (it is Marianne Williamson, after all!) and acknowledged that we were writing within the context of these times. Marianne's beautiful, soulful heart wisdom was like an ever-present perfume beckoning us to a higher level of being. She was a constant reminder to bless our books and the people reading them. She fiercely spoke to the need for us to offer our wisdom in service *now*. Thank you, Marianne, for your welcoming spirit, deep listening, and crystal clarity. Your Line 4 has indeed whispered words that have touched and transformed my life.

Thank you, Ra Uru Hu for receiving the Human Design transmission and sharing it with the world. Your powerful contribution continues to reverberate and awaken humanity.

Thank you Kamud, for introducing to me to Human Design back in 2004. You opened a treasure of riches that continue to impact my life.

Thank you to all the teachers of Human Design who have touched my life with this knowledge and given me the foundation to discover for myself the gift of these teachings.

Writing a book is never a lone venture, and anyone who's written a book knows you can't underestimate the hand of a great editor. Thank you, Erika Roman Saint-Pierre, for recognizing my vision and enthusiastically supporting me to bring it to fruition. I know that after reading the first draft, you said, "It's like you don't even need outside help anymore." Well... I do. You make everything I write shine. I love working with you.

On that note, a big thanks to the keen eyes that combed through the manuscript to catch the errors that accompany writing a piece of work. Thank you, Trevor McKenzie, Teresa Miller, Alexander Lee, Jennet Burghard, Cheryl Campbell, and

Denise Rolland. Thank you, Jennifer Stimpson for the cover design. Thank you to the staff at the Author Incubator who do the all the behind the scene things I don't even know about! And deep gratitude to Lauren Tancredi for always being there for whatever I need.

Thank you to all the staff at the Author Incubator who did everything to make this book come into form. From Lesley Mathews who made sure the book got into the right forms, to Madeline Kosten, who oversaw the whole production, to Jennifer Stimson, who created the book cover. You guys are the unseen heroes!

I've taken big leaps in the last year with my Human Design Practitioner Certification Training for Professionals and could never have written this book without a well of nourishment to balance the flurry of activity. Just about every weekend of 2021 I spent with Greg Toews dropping into *samadhi* with essential oils. Thank you, Greg, Samantha, and Plant Prana, for replenishing my creativity through deep dives into the healing vortex. When I would get stuck with writing, I simply did an oil protocol and answers would arise. I'm looking forward to our collaboration with oils and Human Design. And, I'm looking forward to sharing the essential oil blends you've created to work with the Lines and the Profiles! For Human Design Essential Oil Profiles protocol booklet: robinwinn.com/HDprofiles-essentialoils. To order Human Design Essential Oils for the Profiles: https://plantpranaoils.com/human-design-oils/."

Speaking of the Human Design Practitioner Certification Training, last year, I expanded the program to include An Advanced Practitioner Certification Training. These students, colleagues, family, and friends called forth my experience of Human Design with clients and catapulted me to evolve and share at a new level. Named and unnamed throughout the book, their presence graces these pages. Thank you, Charlotte Friborg, Lauren Tancredi, Kristin Panek, Iris Seng, Anna Rischke, Moudi

Sbeity, Denise Anderson, Heidi Winn, Jennet Burghard, Kelly Ruby Hanson, Tyler Gannon, Vanessa Quiroz, and Cheryl Campbell.

It is a privilege to walk this path with you.

And thank you, to all my students and all the people who have worked with me. I am continuously touched and inspired by you.

I am blessed to have the support of extraordinary groups of people this past year: the Pearls, my Leadership pod, my Women's Circle, My Rockstar group, my HD Coaching pod, and my Pali pod. Thank you, Claire, Debra, Devi, Gwen, Julie, Toni, Anena, Phyllis, Cheryl, Alisha, Letty; Patricia, Laura, Mary, Sheri, Jen; Karinne, Charlotte, Barrie, Jodi, Jo; Nancy, Maggie, Asha, Cari; Debra, Geo, Ane, Marc, Sue, and Yarrow. And always in awe of and grateful to my beloved soul wayfarers – Jane and Gary Bell.

To my multifaceted friends and family, who tolerate and support me as I escape into my *hermitage* and who appreciate that I am doing what I'm called to do. Thank you.

Deep gratitude especially to Charlotte – I honor your path, I value the weave of our worlds, and I appreciate our weekly accountability calls!

And to Deborah, you are a powerful ally and soul friend. I treasure our journey as we step out into the world with our mutative voices.

Big hugs to my sister, Heidi. Your belief in me is steady and enthusiastic! You are a true companion this lifetime.

We stand on the shoulders of giants. I feel that saying reverberating in my bones. Without the kindness of masters that have carried me and shown me the path, I would not have access to the riches of knowledge and tools that are woven into this book. Immeasurable gratitude to Byron Katie, Pali Summerlin, Ammachi, Ram Dass, Lama Palden Drolma, Lama Drupgyu Tenzin, Faisal Muqaddam, Ming Tong Gu, Anat Baniel, Barbara

Kaufman, Leslie Temple-Thurston, Ellen Zucker, Karen Seager, Marion Rosen, Vicki Noble, and Charlene Tschirhart.

A special thanks to my eighty-two-year-old friend and mentor Pali Summerlin. Each time I've written a book, I go through a portal. Writing this third book was unexpectedly challenging. I worked with Pali in retreat and throughout the process to look at and discover the erroneous beliefs and conclusions I drew that shrouded my perceptions. I've had many spiritual openings and awakenings in my lifetime, but the shift in awareness that occurred during the editing process of this book feels like the biggest one to date. It is my version of Byron Katie's cockroach or Eckhart Tolle's park bench. Thank you, Pali, for your sweet and spicy awakening guidance that continues to direct me home.

And finally...

My beloved wife, Yarrow, and our cat, Kali Ma.

Kali, deep soul, you are my co-author. As I write you sit outside my office door in unabashed leisure reminding me to relax. *Let go!* Your steady open awareness and blissful stillness blesses this book. I am so lucky. Thank you.

Yarrow, dear Heart.

Thank you for your patience, your love, and your support.

I could write a whole book of gratitudes just on you.

I adore you. I treasure you. I am so grateful I found my 6/2 soulmate at the tender age of twenty-two.

You are truly a blessing in my life.

ABOUT THE AUTHOR

Robin Winn, LMFT, is the bestselling author of *Understanding Your Clients through Human Design: The Breakthrough Technology* and *Understanding the Centers in Human Design: The Facilitator's Guide to Transforming Pain into Possibility.*

Robin is an innovator, here to expand horizons and help people realize their innate potential.

With a background in Rosen Method Bodywork, Anat Baniel Method NeuroMovement, qigong, Speaking Circles, Diamond

Logos, Tibetan Buddhism, essential oils, and The Work of Byron Katie, Robin brings a rich and deep perspective to life.

After working for twenty-five years as a psychotherapist, Robin was introduced to the Human Design portal. Not only did understanding Human Design dramatically transform her work with clients, but it also opened a new depth of appreciation and compassion in her marriage.

Robin says, "Human Design is alive in me, an ever-deepening recognition of who I am, and a potent reflective medicine that continuously grounds and supports me and the people I work with, to navigate the journey of being human, embodying and embracing our differences, and stepping into our magnificent Selves."

Passionate about the power of Human Design to transform lives, Robin devotes her time training coaches and therapists to use Human Design with their clients. She believes Human Design holds a key to embracing difference and finding a new way forward for humanity.

Robin is a writer, speaker, transformational coach, founder, and director of Human Design Certification Training for Professionals.

She lives on Maui with her wife, Yarrow, and their soulful cat, Kali Ma.

ABOUT DIFFERENCE PRESS

Difference Press is the exclusive publishing arm of The Author Incubator, an educational company for entrepreneurs – including life coaches, healers, consultants, and community leaders – looking for a comprehensive solution to get their books written, published, and promoted. Its founder, Dr. Angela Lauria, has been bringing to life the literary ventures of hundreds of authors-in-transformation since 1994.

A boutique-style self-publishing service for clients of The Author Incubator, Difference Press boasts a fair and easy-to-understand profit structure, low-priced author copies, and author-friendly contract terms. Most importantly, all of our #incubatedauthors maintain ownership of their copyright at all times.

LET'S START A MOVEMENT WITH YOUR MESSAGE

In a market where hundreds of thousands of books are published every year and are never heard from again, The Author Incubator is different. Not only do all Difference Press books reach Amazon bestseller status, but all of our authors are actively changing lives and making a difference.

Since launching in 2013, we've served over 500 authors who came to us with an idea for a book and were able to write it and get it self-published in less than 6 months. In addition, more than 100 of those books were picked up by traditional publishers and are now available in bookstores. We do this by selecting the highest quality and highest potential applicants for our future programs.

Our program doesn't only teach you how to write a book – our team of coaches, developmental editors, copy editors, art directors, and marketing experts incubate you from having a book idea to being a published, bestselling author, ensuring that the book you create can actually make a difference in the world. Then we give you the training you need to use your book to make the difference in the world, or to create a business out of serving your readers.

ARE YOU READY TO MAKE A DIFFERENCE?

You've seen other people make a difference with a book. Now it's your turn. If you are ready to stop watching and start taking massive action, go to http://theauthorincubator.com/apply/.

"Yes, I'm ready!"

OTHER BOOKS BY DIFFERENCE PRESS

The Father, the Son, and the Aha Moment: Tools for Helping You and Your Child Develop a Path to Happiness by Steve & Spencer Barton

Transformational Leadership in Healthcare: The Roadmap to Cultivating a Results-Driven Management Team by Dr. Dorine Fobi-Takusi

Grow Your Recruiting Business: The First 3-Part Blueprint to Create Predictable Profits, Reliable Growth, and Business Freedom by Mike Gionta

GIFT FOR THE READER

Thank you, dear reader, for joining me on this adventure. I am hoping that you've been touched and inspired. I hope that you have a deeper understanding of difference and more capacity to support your clients to thrive.

If you are sparked to continue your journey and deepen your ability to work with people using Human Design, reach out to me at info@clientsandhumandesign.com.

Perhaps you'd be a good fit for our Human Design Practitioner Training program?

Meanwhile, here are some links: the first to download charts for free, the second to download my first book on Understanding Your Clients through Human Design for free, the third to download an audio recording of the meditations, and the last two if you're interested in Human Design and essential oils.

• Download your chart for free chart: https:// clientsandhumandesign.com/free-chart/.

• Download my first book for free: *Understanding Your Clients*

through Human Design: The Breakthrough Technology: https://www.
clientsandhumandesign.com/free-book.

• Contact me at info@clientsandhumandesign.com if you would
like an audio recording of one of the meditations.

• For Human Design Essential Oil Profiles protocol booklet:
http://robinwinn.com/HDprofiles-essentialoils.

• To order Human Design essential oils for the Profiles: https://
plantpranaoils.com/human-design-oils/.

Enjoy your learning path!
Blessings,
Robin

Made in the USA
Las Vegas, NV
11 October 2024